MW01234539

Emotional Abuse

Recognize the Signs of Psychological Abuse and Recovery from Mental Manipulation

Hayden Hanson

Table of Contents

Introduction

E motional abuse is very misunderstood and often thought of as a "mild" form of abuse. It usually goes unrecognized because there are no physical bruises to show for it. It can take any form but is typically recognized through a pattern of intimidation, humiliation, anger, or emotional terrorism—the manipulation of a person's thoughts and emotions by an abuser until they are unable to think clearly or act independently while also feeling ashamed and guilty for being abused.

Now the first question I frequently hear is, "why call it emotional abuse? Because when I think of abuse, I think of physical." However, emotional abuse can be just as damaging, if not more so than physical. Emotional abuse can destroy your self-esteem, mental health and cause you to have major trust issues.

Now let's consider what a pattern is. Many people display abusive behavior at one time or another - and they may even be verbal or emotionally abusive on a daily basis - yet this does not mean they are emotionally abusing the other person. Emotional abuse is usually displayed through a pattern of controlling behaviors designed to manipulate the abuser's partner into doing what he/she wants.

Emotional abusers may make you feel like you are the crazy one. No matter how valid your feelings are or how much he/she was at fault, the abuser will tell you that you overreacted. The abuser will minimize and invalidate your feelings until you doubt yourself and start to believe that you are a "crazy" or over-sensitive person who must be wrong about what is going on in the relationship.

The abuser may even try to convince others of it, including friends, family members, and professionals such as counselors, clergy, or doctors.

It's not uncommon to find out later that a narcissist's most commonly used tool in gaining total control over his victim is other people. If one supports the narcissist, he may find people who can tell or make him believe they support him. This is done especially if the victim has no support system and/or is isolated from friends or family. The abuser will have people in his circle who will bad-mouth and even threaten to expose the victim using any tactic they can think of.

The victim will likely be told that if he leaves the relationship that he is crazy, then at least have a "little respect for him." He may also be threatened with verbal abuse, warnings of harm, or even death threats. (This usually takes place after an attempt to leave. The abuser knows that most abusers will attempt to get their victim back.)

After leaving, the victim is almost always punished. Most abusers spend time looking for new victims while in another relationship. They may act like victims themselves (victim-playing) or even come on strong by appearing to be apologetic and contrite about how bad they were. This is often referred to as "hoovering" after the popular Hoover vacuum cleaners. Just as you can't vacuum up a pile of dust and dirt without first tearing it apart, the abuser will try to find someone who was not completely flattened so they can have another go at destroying an innocent person's sense of self-worth.

Only those who have experienced this type of abuse will know what it is like to be treated so poorly because that type of treatment is reserved only for the abuser's partner - and even then, the abuser may also do such things to his own family members or others he sees as beneath him.

This book will explain the dynamics of various forms of abuse in varying levels in extreme detail and give your insight into how abusers change.

The book will also help you see through his games, recognize his tactics and tell you how to effectively protect yourself from further abuse.

This book is for victims who want to regain control over their lives, reclaim their self-worth, heal and become stronger from the abuse that has been done to them.

It is specifically written for women who have suffered at the hands of emotionally abusive men. It strives to reveal the signs and tell you what is happening; it guides you through the recovery process while helping you understand the behavior.

Chapter 1:

What is Abuse?

Abuse can take various forms and includes not only physical violence but also sexual abuse, emotional abuse, neglect, and financial exploitation.

What is Abuse?

Abuse does not comprise only physical violence but also sexual abuse, emotional abuse, neglect, and financial exploitation.

Common Types of Abuse:

1. Emotional Abuse

Emotional abuse is the most common type of domestic violence that is physical and mental abuse. In the early stages of a relationship, an emotional abuser might try to isolate their partner to prevent them from quitting the relationship or leaving on their own. The emotionally abusive partner might also frequently criticize their partner, and you will find they constantly compare you with others, for example, your ex-boyfriend or ex-girlfriend. If you are upset about something that has happened in your life, these comments will usually be followed by criticism as well.

2. Financial Abuse

Financial abuse is by far the most common type of abuse in relationships. It often takes place alongside other forms of abuse, and it may be that you do not even realize it is taking place. This type of abuse can take many different forms but is usually the misuse of credit cards, burglary, and breaking into bank accounts in order to steal money. This is a type of abuse that the victim does not always realize has taken place until it is too late, for example, when they are either charged with a crime or suddenly find themselves without money to pay for things as a result of the financial abuser's actions.

3. Physical Abuse

Physical abuse is the most commonly accepted type of abuse, and this is when the abuser threatens or uses violence against their partner. Physical abuse can also include destroying property, harming or killing pets, restricting a partner's access to medical care, or forcing them to use drugs or alcohol. This type of abuse can take place at any stage in a relationship and will often escalate over time if the victim does not recognize it for what it is and seek help.

4. Sexual Abuse

Sexual abuse is another very common form of domestic violence that takes place in relationships and can be rape, forcing sex after drugging someone, or sexual harassment such as forcing an unwilling partner to look at pornography.

Why Abuse Happens?

If you have been abused, it is very important to know why the abuse happened and how to prevent it from happening again. Abusers often have a history of abusive behavior that they do not realize until they become involved with an independent partner.

Abuse is a Learned Behavior

Abuse can be learned in many different ways; for example, people who are emotionally abusive were possibly abused themselves when young and learned how to treat others the same way they were treated as a child. To stop abusers from abusing in the future, it is important to understand what makes them behave this way.

When an abuser feels threatened or humiliated, they are more likely to act aggressively.

Abuse is usually a sign that someone feels powerless in their life, but you can empower yourself by leaving the relationship as fast as possible.

It is also important to be aware of the different stages in an abusive relationship, and this is particularly important when considering whether or not to take steps to stop abuse from happening or continuing.

Preventing Abuse:

• Recognizing Red Flags: If you know what some of the signs of abuse are, it will make it easier for you to leave before things get worse than they already are. If there is one thing people regret most, it's that they did not leave a relationship earlier when they had the chance.

• Taking Action: The sooner you leave an abusive relationship, the less likely it is that you will become seriously hurt. If at all possible, leave the relationship immediately if you recognize the signs of abuse for what they are.

• Establishing Boundaries: If you are in an abusive relationship, your partner will most likely be unwilling to accept that their behavior is wrong, and as a result, it will be important for you to establish boundaries with them. You can establish boundaries such as not allowing them to make decisions about money or property without consulting you first and outlining a plan should the abuser decide to become violent.

• Take the First Step: As a victim of abuse, it is important to take the first step of asking for help. It is sometimes too much to ask, but the most important thing you can do is to stay safe and away from your abuser.

Chapter 2:

What are the Signs of Abuse?

How do we know it's emotional abuse? When it is present under its covert nature, emotional abuse is sometimes hard to recognize because it happens in a relationship, in the link between two people. That's why we say that, in its most basic form, emotional abuse equals control. Defining and spotting control issues focuses on the goal of seeking out and stopping emotional abuse.

The signs of emotional abuse can be covert or overt, both to the abuser and the victim.

Overt Signs

Overt signs are the easiest to notice, in which case you may already have an idea of how to define the behavior you're seeing. Overt signs are anything that is outwardly and obviously abusive and damaging, such as yelling or swearing out loud in crowded spaces, like a restaurant, breaking personal property when escalating a dispute, throwing away your belongings, attacking or causing damage to pets, or disappearing for days without notice.

Covert Signs

The abused person often appears frightened of the abuser or fearful of angering or displeasing the abuser. . . . As a result, actions and access are very much controlled, and the person often seems to have no freedom or capacity to make any independent decisions.

Covert emotional abuse tends to take place behind closed doors.

The only outward signs of abuse may be in the behavior of the victim himself, such as displaying:

1. Loss of self-confidence

2. Depression or mental confusion

3. Trouble sleeping

4. Shame and withdrawal behaviors

5. Eating disorders

6. Physical depletion (low energy, extreme weight changes, or an unexplained, repetitive illness)

The use of sex as a tool to abuse others is very frequent; just to avoid an escalating argument that threatens to turn violent, many women will give in and have sex to calm the angry spouse down. Otherwise, they might be accused of being frigid or a lesbian or having affairs with other men. If this shortcut is preferred, it is at the high cost of feeling used as an object or depersonalized by this kind of body abuse.

Behavior that alternates between overt charm and covert cruelty can be very confusing, and it produces a state of disorientation in the spouse who never knows if the person coming through the door will be Dr. Jekyll or Mr. Hyde.

Why is it that, being abused so clearly visible, most people put up with abuse and continue with the relationship?

Some victims are scared of being alone. Often told that they can't survive without a spouse to take care of them, that they dare not try living independently. Moreover, there are still some societies that reject and devalue single women, considering them worthless if they are not able to "keep a man."

Financial and social considerations are giving way, at least in the United States, to a wider perspective on new and different ways of living. The percentage of people living single in individual housing arrangements is growing, which speaks volumes about the acceptance of single living as a respectable and valid option. Nobody is rejected for being single but rather is appreciated as an individual.

Leaving social perspectives aside, the notion that some part of human development must take place alone holds a lot of water. The hidden assumption lurking beneath emotional abuse is, "You are nothing without a partner, and any partner is better than none." This tool for control evaporates into thin air as long as the single person discovers the joy of being able to make decisions in accord with her own deepest desires.

Many victims also believe that society requires them to stay in a toxic relationship, at least "for the children's sake." The tragic result is that children who grow up in an abusive environment tend to accept such as the pattern for their future relationships, hence ensuring another generation follows this toxic cycle.

What are the indications of emotionally abusive behavior?

There are signs that can be discerned by watching the abuser's behavior. Let's say you want to test your partner (or a family member or a friend) for emotionally abusive behavior; ask yourself the following questions- does your partner exhibit ANY of the following behaviors?

- Frequently humiliates you based on your intelligence, personality, skills, or appearance

- Ridicules your opinions and ideas in public

- Put up a fuss about or physically stops you from seeing your family and friends

- Steamrolls over you during heated debates so that the blame is displaced onto you

- Controls the finances and hides his own expenses from you

- Shifts debt to you because of a made-up "obligation" to pay them

- Guilt-trips, threatens, insults, or otherwise obligates you into having sex

- Denies you sexual intimacy as punishment

- Threatens or harms your personal possessions (inanimate or animate, such as pets)

- Threatens or harms your children

- Insults you and then says, "It was just a joke."

- Humiliates you in public or in front of your or his friends

- Belittles you for holding certain beliefs or for your heritage

- Makes insulting comments about your race or social class

- Purposely denies you affection or approval when you ask for it

- Changes the subject or rolls his/her eyes during a "This is how I feel" conversation

- Gives you the silent treatment or simply walks away from you

- Threatens you with blackmail or secrets

- Seems to enjoy/get off on fighting and arguments

- Has a public "facade" and behavior that no one else but you see through

- Threatens you if you do something (intentional or not) to ruin his/her public image

- Tries to control your appearance (the way you dress or do your hair)

- Threatens to leave or throw you out

- Treats you like a servant or his property

- Lies or manipulates the truth to make you look bad

- Carries on affairs and/or harasses you about imagined affairs to shift the attention

- Tells you what to do instead of requesting

- Blames you or others for all his problems

- Acts oblivious to other people's feelings yet expects attention for the slightest instance of having his feelings hurt

- Says or promises good things (professing love, saying romantic things) but does things that hurt

Any of these behaviors, when exhibited repeatedly, constitute emotionally abusive behavior that causes psychological stress or trauma for the victim. They are about keeping the other person weak and under the control of the abuser.

A woman named Clara posted this in a forum for the emotionally abused, "I was going to nursing school, and each day was a discovery trip for my brain. I'd get back home and share my new ideas with my husband, only to have him dissect and destroy them with his "logical arguments. Only after several repetitions of this discouraging behavior did I learn to keep my ideas to myself. What was really a big surprise was to hear him, at a party four weeks later, explaining those same ideas to his friends, as if they were his own reflections!. Then and there, I understood how my own excitement about learning, going to school again, having my brain alive with theories, etc., was so threatening to him! What he was doing was trying to keep the learning of my brain under his control, so he was not left behind!"

However, perhaps this list of emotional abuse indicators is missing something. It is not exhaustive. Perhaps your suspicion about your partner is based on a particular action or behavior of his that is hard to define or pin down. Trust your own perceptions because if it feels painful, diminishing you, or somehow humiliating you, be sure that it is not a behavior intended to make you feel good, or support your growth.

Chapter 3:

The Effects of Emotional Abuses

W hen victims realize aggression, they experience shock. Up to this point, they do not suspect anything; perhaps they are even too trusting.

They feel confused and offended and feel everything "collapsed." The extent of the injury depends on the degree of surprise and the unpreparedness for the consequences of the perverse effect. During an emotional shock, the victim mixes feelings of suffering and anxiety; there is a feeling of violent interference, shock, powerlessness, and collapse, which some victims describe as psychic aggression: "It's like a fist punch!", "He said terrible words to me, and I feel like a boxer who is already on the floor, but they continue to beat him mercilessly."

Strange, but anger and indignation are rare, even after the victims decide to part with the aggressor. And anger could help liberation. Victims will complain about the injustice of their fate, but nevertheless, they will not rebel. Anger will appear later, and most often, it will be restrained, which means it will not be effective. To experience real, liberating anger, the victim needs to not be under the influence of the aggressor.

When victims begin to realize that they are being manipulated, they feel cheated, as if they were being targeted. They get the feeling that they were misled, that they are not respected. A little later, they finally became convinced that they were victims, that they had been manipulated, and lost their self-esteem because of that. They are ashamed of the actions provoked by the manipulation: "I had to start resisting earlier!", "Why didn't I see anything?"

Shame comes from realizing their pathological indulgence, which made possible violence on the part of the partner.

Sometimes people want to avenge themselves, but more often, they try to rehabilitate themselves, to restore their self-esteem. They expect an apology from their aggressor, which will not be.

Weakening of Protective Functions

When the stupor that the victim experiences during the period of perverse influence recedes, the person begins to feel obvious aggression. The protective abilities of a person are not unlimited; they gradually decrease. After a certain amount of stress, the ability to adapt disappears, and mental exhaustion sets in, more prolonged and more severe disorders occur.

Basically, it is at the stage of decompensation that victims come to us, psychiatrists. They have a general state of anxiety, psychosomatic disorders, or depression. In more impulsive people, decompensation can be expressed in the transition to violent actions, which can bring them to a psychiatric hospital. In the eyes of the aggressor, these disorders often seem to be an excuse for moral persecution.

It is surprising that, at this stage, when we offer employees who are persecuted in the workplace to stop work for a while, they very rarely agree: "If I stop work, it will be even worse! It will cost me dearly!" Fear makes you put up with everything and anything.

Such a depressive state is associated with mental exhaustion, with an excess of stress. Victims feel exhaustion, tiredness, and apathy. They are not interested in anything. They are unable to focus even on the simplest actions. They may have thoughts of suicide. The risk is especially great at the moment when the victims realize that they have been deceived and that nothing will help them regain the fullness of their minds. If, in such cases, suicide or attempted suicide occurs, this supports the perverted people's confidence that the partner was weak, that her mind was clouded, or that she was initially crazy, and that the aggression made her feel justified.

During aggression, a perverted person behaves in such a way as to appear omnipotent, demonstrating moral rigor and prudence. Because of this, the process of losing illusions about the partner exacerbates the state of the victim. In general, life events that can lead to a state of depression include not only the death of a loved one or a divorce but also the loss of an ideal or an overvalued idea. As a result, there is a feeling of uselessness, powerlessness, and defeat. The starting point leading to a state of depression is likely to be a feeling of defeat and powerlessness, humiliation and feeling cornered, then a difficult or dangerous situation.

During the moral persecution after the failure of numerous attempts to establish a dialogue with the aggressor, the victim experiences a state of permanent anxiety, which is supported by ceasing attacks. This condition precedes the onset of fear and constant expectation, the cure of which often requires additional medication.

In some victims, the reaction manifests itself physiologically (gastric ulcer, cardiovascular, skin diseases, etc.). The body responds to an encroachment on the psyche of the victim, which she did not suspect, but could lead to the destruction of her personality. Some people brought to this state lose weight and weaken. Psychosomatic disorders are not a direct result of aggression but a person's inability to resist it (no matter what a person does, it will be wrong, she will always be to blame).

The reaction of some victims comes down to a change in behavior that is a direct result of perverse provocations. This is expressed in vain attempts to force oneself to hear (for example, nervous attacks in public) or in violent actions against the aggressor, which will only serve as an excuse for the latter: "I warned you, he/she is in a terrible state!"

It is known that impulsive aggressiveness can lead to a cruel crime to the same extent as a predatory one, but it seems that people with an impulsive type of aggression are more at risk of committing a crime. Perverted people, to prove how bad their victim is, are ready to provoke in her violence directed against themselves.

Another consequence that is often neglected is the dissociation of personality (the more well-known term is "split personality.")

In the reference book of the Department of Natural Sciences, dissociation (bifurcation) of a person is defined as a violation of functions that, in the normal state, are not separable from each other, such as consciousness, memory, self-identification, or perception of the environment. This is a phenomenon of protection from fear, grief, or powerlessness after any traumatic event, which is so alien to a normal perception that the psyche either transforms it or expels it from the human mind. With the dissociation of personality, there is a separation of what can be endured and what cannot be endured, leading to amnesia. The experience gained is filtered, thus bringing relief or partial protection.

The phenomenon of dissociation enhances the perverse effect and presents an additional difficulty that must be taken into account during therapy.

A Break-Up

Victims can respond in two ways to an increasingly clear threat: they submit to and acknowledge the superiority of the aggressor, allowing him to calmly continue his destructive activities; rebel and fight to leave. Submitting to too strong or too old influence, some people are not able to fight or leave. Sometimes they can consult a psychiatrist or psychotherapist, but at the same time immediately refuse any fundamental research. They just want to "hold the blow," transfer their enslavement without any special consequences and "save face." These people usually prefer medication. However, after a series of depressions, an overdose of tranquilizers, and toxic substances that can occur in the human body, and the psychiatrist will be forced to offer psychotherapy again.

Parting, if at all possible, always takes place at the initiative of the victim. The process of liberation from the aggressor is accompanied by bitterness and guilt on the part of the former victim, as perverted narcissistic people pretend to be abandoned victims, and in this, they find a new reason for violence. When a relationship is broken, perverted people consider their interests infringed and become picky, taking advantage of the fact that victims, trying to quickly end this process, are still ready to make any concessions.

In a couple, blackmail and pressure are carried out through the children, if any, or through court procedures regarding joint properties. In a professional environment, a case is often brought against a victim who can always be blamed for something, for example, if a person accidentally took home an important document. In any case, the aggressor complains that his interests are infringed on, although, in reality, it is the victim who loses everything.

Evolution

If the victim nevertheless succeeds at the cost of his own efforts to finally break off relations with the aggressor, it is still impossible to deny the dramatic consequences of the earlier life, in which the victim was reduced to the state of things. From this moment on, any memory or new event will be seen through the tinted lenses of her past experience.

The physical distance from the aggressor at first brings the victim a sense of freedom: "Finally, I can breathe freely!" After a period of shock, interest in work or leisure activities, curiosity towards the world or people, and other feelings still blocked by addiction reappear with time away from the aggressor. However, it is not without difficulties.

Some victims of moral persecution come out of it, only retaining bad memories that they can control, mainly cases of short exposure or violence outside the family. Many experience unpleasant moments of reminiscence of traumatic situations but put up with them.

Attempts to forget more often lead to the appearance of belated mental or somatic disorders, as if you suffered it through another's body, while the psyche was active and inaccessible to the influence of the aggressor.

Experienced violence can leave light consequences that practically do not interfere with normal social life. The victims' psyche seems unscathed, but at the same time, less specific symptoms remain, such as an attempt to conceal the experienced aggression.

Chapter 4:

Psychological Abuse

P sychological abuse is a form of abuse where the victim is exposed to psychological trauma. One of the challenges with psychological violence is that, unlike physical violence, there might not be physical scars as evidence. Psychological abuse happens each time the victim is subjected to emotional distress. In many cases, psychological abuse is accompanied by verbal or physical abuse.

Many people are victims of psychological abuse at some point in time, but they are never aware of it. Without proper understanding of yourself and what your life is about, you might never know when you are under attack. It also becomes difficult to come up with effective strategies you can use to cope with the trauma from such abuse.

While anyone is susceptible to this kind of abuse, women and children are the most affected by psychological abuse. The attacks target perceptions, feelings, and thoughts. Psychological abuse might not be physical, but the effect on the victim's persona is just as bad.

In a relationship with a narcissistic partner, there are several symptoms, reactions, and conditions that the victim might experience, which are signs of abuse. The narcissist conditions the victim by creating experiences in relationships, which have a negative impact on the victim. Here are some of the signs you might be suffering psychological abuse in your relationship:

- Intense insecurities – your abuser identifies your personal insecurities and, over time, uses them to put you down. Your insecurities grow stronger, and you cannot trust anyone.

- Disbelief in yourself – many victims' lives change for the worse because they no longer believe in themselves. Your confidence is eroded to a point where you can no longer trust your judgment.

- Incapability – victims of abuse who were once assured and competent in everything they do suddenly become incapable and uncertain about everything.

- Anxiety – you live a life of uncertainty and fear. You are constantly afraid something bad will happen. You don't trust good things because you believe the happiness is short-lived, and the worst is just right around the corner. You also feel emotionally drained and incapable of enjoying true happiness.

- Indecision – victims who were once grounded become indecisive, confused, and unable to trust anyone, not even themselves.

- Esteem issues – psychological abuse erodes your confidence. You cannot see yourself as anything better than what your abuser says you are. You shy away from the public, afraid that everyone sees the weaknesses in you.

These are the effects of psychological abuse. They manifest in different ways, but one thing is certain about them – they erode the very core of your being, your personality. If you cannot recognize yourself, how can someone else?

Psychological violence is meted out to victims in different categories. We will address five of the spheres of life where healthy relationships are important and how narcissists take everything away from you.

Children and Families

- Trust issues

Life is one big frightening place for a child raised by narcissists. Strings are attached to everything, especially love. Children need unconditional love; however, children of narcissistic parents grow up learning that there is always something attached to it. Such children grow up suspicious of affection. It becomes difficult for them to trust anyone, especially those who are getting too close to them (Keene & Epps, 2016).

Interestingly enough, while such children struggle to embrace genuine affection, they are drawn to toxic relationships and affection. This happens because the feelings shared in such relationships are those that are too familiar, they can relate. Toxic relationships become a comfortable place for such children.

It is easier for a child brought up in a narcissistic environment to trust a bad person disguised as their savior than it is for them to trust someone who is genuine and offers emotional stability.

Toxic people are an embodiment of the same challenges the children endured when growing up. Because their minds have been conditioned to embrace such instances, they are not afraid to interact with toxic people. They learn not to trust or not to trust too much – this is easier because they have done it all their life.

- Inability to commit

Children raised in a narcissistic environment struggle with commitment issues. When you meet them, at first glance, they seem like they are looking to establish commitment with someone. However, deep down, they fear commitment. These kids grow up alienated by the people closest to them, so it is difficult to commit to someone or something. Commitment for such children is often based on what feels right at the moment, not because they really want to commit.

Long-term relationships are not easy to get into because the feeling of being tied down to something is odd. When they encounter someone who truly loves them, it is unsettling because they have to open up about their vulnerabilities to this person, and they are not sure whether this person will stay or walk away. When you grow up alienated by family, stability and forever relationships become a fallacy to you.

Commitment to someone for such a child means that they are giving up control of their lives. Someone else is in charge of their emotions. Naturally, such children will go into defense mode to protect themselves from being hurt. They know the feeling; they have lived through it and cannot risk it again. When facing the prospect of an intense relationship, it is easier to withdraw, even without a reason. They find it easier to give up on someone who loves them than be with them and experience unconditional love.

- Hyperactive attunement

Hyperactivity is one of the symptoms victims of abuse learn to help them cope with their abuser. It helps them know when things are about to get messy. They are keen on subtle changes in the way the abuser responds to them. This makes them realize changes in facial expression, tone, and so forth. They can also identify contradictions between gestures and spoken words.

It is so exhausting to learn all this as a child. However, it is also important for them because it is the only survival technique they are aware of, which can help them avoid unnecessary pain. They grow up on the lookout for verbal, physical, and emotional cues from narcissistic parents and caregivers.

This defense mechanism helps them get through a lot and protects them from the unknown. However, it also breeds a sense of prediction, which can be very unsettling for someone who is genuine but does not know how to align their words and gestures. For the child, it might be impossible to control how people react, but they can use this technique to choose the relationships they can cultivate or end.

- Afraid of intimacy

Intimacy is an emotional minefield for children raised by narcissists. When they try to open up, it is easier to share too much about their struggles hoping that someone might genuinely feel and ease their pain. The challenge here is that they often end up with toxic narcissists whose only desire is to prey on their weaknesses and exploit them for everything they have.

This is one of the reasons why such children are afraid of intimacy later on in life. Intimacy requires that you open up to your partner. You have to be vulnerable around one another. You must allow your partner to see you for who you are, with all your weaknesses, embrace you, and love you endlessly.

Exposure to so much hurt while growing up destroys the concept of intimacy for these children. Instead of allowing someone the chance to hurt them, it is easier to cut them off, close all avenues leading to their emotions (Yates, 2010). They crave intimacy like everyone else, but it is so huge a risk. At times the prospect of opening up to intimacy brings back nasty memories, and it is easier to forget about intimacy altogether.

- Affinity for toxic relationships

Toxic relationships are normal for children raised by narcissists. They have a lot of experience in this, and it is easier to embrace these relationships because they almost always know what to expect. They embrace abuse as a normal thing, and that is why they find it easier to entertain people who belittle or envy them.

In early adulthood or later on in life, when they take stock of their friendships and relationships, they realize they have so many toxic people in their lives that they are comfortable around. This happens because they share a bond. The struggle is all too familiar; it is the only thing they know.

- Emotional sabotage

Narcissistic parents create an unhealthy relationship with their children. Children grow up afraid. They know one thing leads to another and are pessimistic about situations. Respect and true love are foreign to them. If they come across someone who loves them unconditionally, it can be unsettling.

What does it even mean to be loved without expecting something back? How does someone even do that? This crisis sets the stage for emotional sabotage. Unconsciously, the child finds a way to sabotage that relationship because it is too good to be real. The defense mechanism for these kids is usually that anything that cannot come too close to them cannot harm them.

It is okay to protect yourself, but at times it comes at a price. Many opportunities are lost, opportunities for learning, growth, careers, and personal intimate relationships.

The following are some of the signs of emotional abuse that you need to be aware of in a relationship with a narcissist:

- Rationalizing the abuse

Abuse in a relationship hurts on so many levels. Victims of narcissists usually end up normalizing the abuse to the point where they deny it happening in the first place. You minimize and rationalize the problem. This is a survival mechanism that helps the victim dissociate from the pain of abuse. You get to a point where you feel your abuser is not a bad person. They had to react the way they did because you probably did something terrible to provoke them.

- Fear of success

Narcissists do not just take away your happiness, they take away your life. At some point, you stop doing the things you used to love. Success becomes a myth for you because it makes you happy, yet your partner hates it when you derive happiness from anything other than themselves. Talent, happiness, joy, and everything else that interests you become a source of darkness, reprimand, and reprisal.

As this continues, you become depressed, lose confidence, anxiety sets in, and you learn to hide away from the spotlight, allowing your partner to shine instead. What your abuser is doing is not keeping you away from your wins because they feel you are not good enough; they do it because they are afraid your success will weaken their hold on you.

- Self-destruction and sabotage

A victim of narcissistic abuse replays the words and actions in their mind all the time until it becomes second nature. You learn to associate certain actions in the relationship with violence and reprimand. You almost expect a negative reaction from your partner each time you do something. This amplification of negativity grows into self-sabotage, and if your partner is a malignant narcissist, suicide might not be so far off.

Chapter 5:
Sexual Abuse

D oes your partner try to force you through words or actions to engage in sexual activity against your will? Does he force himself on you, even when you say "No"? If so, this is a form of harassment and abuse.

If your partner tries to make you (through physical force, threats, insults, guilt trips, etc.) engage in sexual acts that you don't feel comfortable with, this is also sexual harassment and abuse. If any sexual advances are unwanted, and you make it known that they are unwanted and want it to stop, but he or she continues, then it's harassment.

Some abusers assume they have sexual "rights" to their partner, whether or not the partner agrees to the sexual encounter. The abuser cajoles, guilt-trips, shames, or does whatever it takes to coerce or force the victim into sexual activity. This sometimes includes forced sex.

In fact, until 1975, every state in the United States had a "marital exemption" that allowed a husband to rape his wife without fear of legal consequences. Since 1993, all 50 states have enacted laws against marital rape, but, even so, it is still difficult to prove spousal rape.

Please note that spousal or intimate partner rape is a form of physical violence that goes beyond just manipulation and psychological coercion. If sexual harassment has turned into forced sexual acts, please contact the National Domestic Abuse Hotline, law enforcement, or your counselor to get the support you need.

Using sex to manipulate, control, embarrass or shame the person who is supposed to be your most intimate partner is the ultimate act of selfishness and disrespectfulness. It can be one of the most damaging forms of emotional (and physical) abuse. The following are scripts to stop sexual abuse:

Pressuring You to Have Sex

I want you to stop harassing me to have sex. For sex to be enjoyable for me, we need to be in a loving and kind space together. Pressuring and shaming make me want to avoid sex altogether. When you treat me with love, kindness, and respect, that's when I want to have sex with you.

Crossing Your Sexual Boundaries

I do not feel comfortable doing that, and I never will. Stop trying to force or cajole me into doing it now and forever. Respect my boundaries so that we can have a good sex life, or we'll need to go to counseling to figure it out.

Demeaning You During Sex

You may not demean me or make insulting comments about my body during sex. That is deeply unkind and hurtful, and I won't stand for it. I cannot be intimate with someone who speaks this way to me.

Threatening to Cheat on You

Stop threatening to cheat on me when I don't feel like having sex. I am not available to you every moment you want sex. I'm your partner, not just a sexual outlet for you. If you need more sex, we can go to counseling to talk about how to improve our sex life. But threatening affairs will only make things worse between us.

Chapter 6:

Types of Emotional Abuse

O nce you have gotten accustomed to spotting the traits and characteristics of the emotionally abusive person, it will become easy to spot them. You will also start to notice that you feel drained when you are around them. This will help teach you about the different traits, characteristics, and types of emotional abuse.

Psychological abuse can be found everywhere. It can happen amongst friends, at work, in schools, in relationships, and in family life. You can't escape it. These abusers are out there, and it's very hard to avoid them. But it is possible to identify them from the way they act. This is why it is so important to be on the alert and understand how to interpret their actual intentions. These abusive people are also known as toxic people. They are draining and hard to deal with and leave you feeling used.

Scholars and psychologists aren't totally sure how to evaluate them because these abusers are far from suffering from a mental illness. In the majority of cases, they create damage by using the power they have over others.

There are many red flags to help warn you and make sure that you don't get trapped by another emotionally abusive person. The first things we are going to look at are these warnings.

Parental Abuse

This is probably a type of abuse that you don't want to think about, but it happens and is fairly common. This can include abuse from stepparents, guardians, grandparents, and anybody else that is a parental figure in a child's life. Here's an example: Grandma Jean came to visit and made some comments about her granddaughter, how fat she was looking, and how she dresses. While the comments are infrequent and it might not seem like abuse at first, the derogatory statements are abuse. Grandma isn't doing much to help the child gain confidence; instead, she is taking it away from her.

Hurtful and offhanded comments, like the ones from the example, are just one instance where abuse doesn't actually require a pattern from a single person. Children tend to be more sensitive to things like this, and such comments leave a lasting impression when they happen over a long period of time and on a regular basis. In fact, the more people say certain things to a child, the more they are affected.

Constant negative comments aimed towards different personality traits from physical appearance to behavior have a lasting impression on a child. While it's sad how frequently this abuse happens between parents and children, what's worse is the complicated reason behind the abuse. Parents who berate their children with the reason for causing harm are disturbed people. Chances are, though, the parent doesn't actually hate their child. Their hurtful remarks are likely due to incompetence.

For example, if a child is a little heavier or they have developed a few unhealthy habits, their parent's comments could be their warped way of expressing their concern about their wellbeing. This is ineffective and harmful, but, unfortunately, harshness and insults are the only things that some people understand. There's actually a good chance that the parents were raised with these types of insults as well.

This likely has you all wondering where parenting fits into things. Where is the line drawn between abuse and a strict parent? First off, discipline is important in a child's life. The right kind of discipline can create a strong character and teach right from wrong. To positively discipline a child, you have to teach them to respect rules and have strong values, a sense of morality, and a strong work ethic. Well-disciplined children are safer in the world as adults.

For some parents, strict parenting means creating a rigid daily routine for all their activities. Providing a child with a no-budge schedule is most often considered strict, but it isn't abuse. Discipline becomes abusive when the consequences and punishment from infractions turn inconsistent, excessive, and focus on causing fear instead of teaching them valuable lessons.

Abusive parents won't think much about how they discipline their child, and the punishments that they inflict will often be on a whim. Rather than explaining what they did wrong, the punishments are outbursts and little more than psychological torture or deprivation. The most common feature of an abusive home environment is unpredictability.

Relationship Abuse

Emotional abuse happens a lot between parent and child, but it also happens in other relationships with friends, spouses, or boyfriend/girlfriend. Most of the time, the person being abused isn't new to it. They likely faced emotional abuse as a child.

Let's not forget that men can be victims as well. TV, movies, social media, and the like seem to put emphasis on women being abused. It's important to make sure women get help, but something we don't see a lot of is how men are susceptible to being emotionally abused. Society has conditioned us to believe that men are always strong and never bullied, but it happens more than we think.

The problem is, though, a man being emotionally abused by a woman is more stigmatized than physical abuse. This is why most men won't report psychological terror.

Female-specific spousal abuse isn't all that different from male-specific. The one thing women tend to do more than a man is use sex as a weapon of control. In some extreme cases, the woman might threaten the man with accusations of rape.

I'm by no means trying to lessen what women face; I just want to shed some light on the other side of the story. When this type of abuse starts in a marriage, it tends to begin with one spouse trying to make things easier, and this causes them to isolate themselves.

Besides the common forms of control, men are more capable of causing specific types of emotional abuse. This is especially true for inflicting fear and threats of violence.

Both men and women, when abusive, will belittle, humiliate and withhold affection from their partner. They try to control the relationships their partners have outside of the marriage as well. This type of behavior can last for years. Only when one spouse moves on or is pushed too far, do they realize that trauma has taken place.

The most common cause of spousal abuse is a broken home. This isn't true for all, but it is common. The abuse is not your fault, and an important step in healing is to instill this truth in your mind. It's easy to become complacent, to just accept what is going on, and believe you can't do anything to change it, but you can stop it and heal.

Now, marriage isn't the only place emotional abuse can happen. It can occur in any relationship. This tends to be harder to notice, but then something changes within the relationship.

When it comes to abusive friendships, a lot of people underestimate how damaging the abuse can be. This is because friendships are viewed as things that can be easily disposed of, more so than marriages. True friends are not that common anymore and have turned into a wide circle of acquaintances. This means that friendships can be easily found but take years to build.

This is what makes misinterpreting an abusive friendship for a true friend so dangerous. The need for a friend causes a blind spot and leaves you holding onto a person who is only interested in using you for personal gain. They are nice when they need something, but it changes when you become less useful. This type of tainted friendship can happen to anybody, especially those who are considered "social butterflies."

Just because you may not be socially active doesn't mean that you have to settle for a person who belittles you and calls you names. Plus, it's a truth of life that it is better to be alone than be with a person who abuses you. This might sound harsh, but you'll find more success once you stop allowing yourself to be used by others who don't care about you. You will then start to attract those who actually care.

Rejecting

A common trait of emotionally abusive people is rejecting their victim. A partner, parent, friend, or caregiver who displaces this type of behavior toward another will let their victim know, in different ways, that they aren't wanted. Belittling a person or putting down their worth are some ways that this type of emotional abuse manifests. Other types of rejecting can include telling a person to leave or, worse, calling them names, making them a scapegoat, or blaming them for other people's problems. Refusing to hold a child as they are growing or refusing to talk to another person are also abusive behaviors.

Ignoring

Adults who haven't really had their emotional needs met will find it hard to respond to the needs of others, especially their own children. They may not be able to attach to others or provide a positive nurturing experience for their child. They might not show any interest in a person, or they withhold affection, or might not even acknowledge that another person is present. They are likely physically there but are completely emotionally unavailable. Failing to respond to another is emotional abuse.

Terrorizing

People who curse, yell, and threaten their child, spouse, or friend are doing serious psychological damage. Now, we talked about yelling earlier. Yelling and cursing are fine if it is temporary and the cause of it is addressed, and you have a healthy conversation about what made them upset. Cursing and yelling at another person constantly or for no reason is where it becomes abuse.

Singling out a person and ridiculing them for normal emotional reactions is abusive. Threatening a person with abandonment, physical harm, harsh words, or in severe cases, death is completely unacceptable. Even if you are joking, causing a person to be terrified by intimidation or threats is some of the worst emotional abuse. When it comes to children, this includes knowing, hearing, or witnessing abuse within the home.

Isolating

This is a common abuse tactic by parents. When parents use isolation, they may not let their children engage in normal activities with their peers. They may keep a baby in their room, unexposed to external stimulation, or they can prevent their teen from participating in extracurricular activities. Requiring somebody to stay in their room from the time they get home from school until they go to school the next day, restricting what they eat, or forcing them to stay away from friends and family can be very destructive, depending on the severity and circumstances.

Corrupting

People who are corruptive to others may allow their child to partake in drugs or alcohol or may enable the user. They talk others into treating animals cruelly or participate in criminal activities like gambling, prostitution, assault, stealing, and so on. Abusive parents might let their children watch inappropriate content for their age. Encouraging others to do things that are harmful or illegal is abusive and needs to be reported.

Chapter 7:

Abusive Relationship vs. Healthy Relationship

E very relationship is different - each one has its own beauty, as well as its own imperfections. Since the dawn of mankind, human beings have survived and thrived due to social companionship - whether those are through tribes, communities, families, or partners.

It is in our nature to seek companionship to feel safe and fulfilled, and romantic relationships are often the most sought out form of companionship. People usually crave having someone to share things with and to grow old with; knowing they have someone in their corner.

The basis of being in a relationship is usually to find true love, a great friend, and happiness. However, like most things in life, relationships also come with their own challenges. Even though a relationship entails two souls coming together to care for each other and love each other, these souls are still individual people with their own personalities, core values, and beliefs.

No matter how similar or different these two people are, the way they conduct and maintain their relationship will determine whether or not it is a healthy one.

It is sometimes confusing to know whether the relationship you are in is, in fact, healthy or not. Each person has their own preferences, tolerances, vices, etc.

Who is to say what the universal definition of a happy relationship is? While the meaning of a happy relationship may differ from person to person, there are several universal truths that determine whether your relationship is healthy or unhealthy:

Being Content Within Yourself

For one to achieve a healthy relationship, you need to have a healthy relationship with yourself first. This means loving yourself unconditionally and feeling whole. It all starts with you.

We are constantly growing and changing, but before we get into a relationship with somebody, we should know who we are, what we want from life, and what we want in a relationship.

We should feel confident about ourselves and be willing to be our authentic selves with another person. Being content with yourself means being able to validate yourself instead of seeking validation from someone else.

If you aren't whole and happy with yourself, your glass is only half full. If two people come together expecting the other person to fill up their glass, they may be disappointed, as the other person may not have that much to give from their glass either.

This can turn into an unhealthy codependent relationship that exhausts both parties.

Understanding What True Love Actually Looks Like

Love is a concept that many of us wish to bring to life but may not fully understand. We might think we know what true love is based on past relationships, romance movies, and novels, or simply from what people tell us. What true love actually is, is a choice. It is the choice we make to love someone wholeheartedly every day. While love is based on emotion, a choice is based on logic and reason. It is easy to fall in love with someone quickly because your emotions take over, and you are addicted to that temporary feeling of happiness. However, once the romance and honeymoon period fades, which it will, true love will be determined by your CHOICE to keep loving this person through thick and thin. A choice based on reason and logic.

If we can choose to remain close to our best friends, we can apply the same principle to our relationships - we can choose to love them every day, come what may. No relationship will constantly be magical and perfect; there will be times when you really question whether you want to keep going. At those times, the relationships that survive are the ones that are built from two people choosing to truly love each other every day regardless. True love is when two people consciously know everything about each other (the good and the bad) and still choose to love each other and be with each other. Of course, this does not mean that you forgive your partner for abusive behavior and choose to stay with them regardless of how they treat you. True love also means respecting each other, and if you are not being respected, then your relationship is probably not very healthy.

If you ever asked an elderly couple what kept them together all these years, they would probably say it is acceptance and understanding. They have made the decision to be with each other, taking into consideration every single aspect of the other person. They have accepted who their partner is and understand the way they operate. Only when you are able to accept and understand the other person are you able to use your logical reasoning to decide whether you want to be with this person. Paradoxically, logic is what makes your love true and pure.

Accepting Your Partner for Who They Truly Are

Healthy relationships involve two people loving each other wholeheartedly, which means that they also accept each other for the way they are.

The first step is to accept yourself, flaws and all. Self-love is the key to having a healthy relationship with someone else. If you are able to accept yourself, you can be content within yourself.

When you are content from within, you are capable of accepting your partner for the way they are and will not expect them to change either.

Of course, if there are tiny aspects about your partner (or about you) that can be discussed and changed for the betterment of the relationship, that is totally understandable and healthy.

However, if you are unhappy with who your partner is at their very core, in terms of their values, beliefs, and personality, you are going to have an unhappy relationship because you will constantly try to change them.

This can lead to consistent disappointment and feeling short-changed, while your partner could feel resentment towards you and insecure with themselves.

If you truly love someone for who they are, you would not want to change them. It is as simple as that.

Being Honest and Respectful

This goes without saying - honesty and respect are extremely vital in a healthy relationship. When you and your partner are able to be completely honest with each other and respect each other in every way, only then will your relationship make you feel secure and happy. When you both are honest with each other, you are coming from a place of emotional maturity. There will be times when the truth may not be something neither of you wants to hear, but the fact that it is being laid out shows that you respect each other and you want what is best for the other person.

Open communication is essential to making your relationship work, and if honesty is met with an emotional reaction, that may harm your relationship more than help. When someone is being honest with you, they are taking a big step and letting you in on the truth, even when it hurts. By doing this, they are respecting you enough to make sure you are not in the dark, oblivious to the truth. They believe that you are able to handle the truth and are able to tell you anything. At this point, it is best to show that person respect rather than react with emotion because they are taking a big step by being honest.

In emotionally abusive relationships, when the abuser is feeling insecure or reacts with emotion, they exhibit defensiveness to the person being honest, and this usually results in a conflict, as they perceive this honesty to be an attack on their character. These kinds of arguments are based solely on insecurity and emotional reaction when the conversation should be a healthy conversation about what was said. The more someone reacts to honesty rather than listens, the less their partner will be inclined to be honest in the future, as they will gravitate towards avoiding conflict. This is where relationships become toxic and unhealthy, as couples start to hide things from each other. Thus, it is important that partners respect each other and take a few breaths before responding to whatever is being said so that a productive and positive conversation can take place.

There Should Be Mutual Trust

If you do not trust each other, then you do not have a healthy relationship. Being committed to someone means sharing a big part of your life with this person. Aspects of your life become intertwined, and this person becomes extremely important to you.

If you do not trust them, either because of their character or because of emotional wounds, you may have yet to heal, that could lead to a lot of pain. If you get anxious when your partner goes out with their friends without you, or you check their phone regularly, then you have low levels of trust in your partner.

Mutual trust brings partners closer together, as both of you feel secure and safe with the other person. If this is not the case, you both can try to build your trust for the other. However, this only works if both partners are willing to work at it and be understanding of the other person's vulnerabilities.

Taking Responsibility for Your Own Feelings

Your partner will most likely push your buttons, and it is important to recognize when this happens. In a healthy relationship, you should be able to take responsibility for what you are thinking and how you feel because you and only you are in charge of how you react to situations. For example, if your partner hurls a hurtful comment at you and you get upset, the first step is to recognize that getting upset is the reaction you chose to have. It is okay to feel what you feel, but from there, it is vital to think about what you can do to relieve that emotion or thought - whether it is taking some space to cool off or talking to your partner about it in a constructive manner.

Unhealthy relationships involve the person who has been hurt blaming their partner for their feelings. Their partner may be the trigger or the situation that caused them to have a reaction, but they did not dictate how the person should have felt, and vice versa. The person is choosing to feel this way and also choosing whether they want to stew in that feeling or to find a way to resolve it and let it go. It's not the easiest thing to do, but with practice, it becomes an automatic behavior.

Chapter 8:

How to Leave an Abusive Relationship?

O ne of the things that you have to realize is that a narcissist does not see the need to seek help from a therapist because, after all, they think that there is nothing wrong with them. Recovery is for those who have been through abuse. If you have been or are in a relationship with a narcissist, it is high time you left and sought help from a professional. It is this kind of support that you need to rebuild your self-confidence and bounce back to your self-esteem.

Trust me; you are better than you have ever thought possible. The narcissist might have managed to puncture your self-confidence and even crushed your self-esteem, but most importantly, you are just a victim. You are not unworthy like they want you to believe. Finding a health professional with a specialty in trauma recovery will help you journey through the healing process to recovery. If you are not able to leave the relationship, a therapist can also help you to learn the best ways in which you can communicate effectively with your abuser so that you can set boundaries that they will respect and hence, protect you so that they will no longer take advantage of you.

Here are some of the steps that you will have to go through to help you journey through healing to recovery:

Step 1: Cut Contact

Once you have left the relationship, keep it at that! Stop maintaining contact with your abuser. The main reason why you left is that the situation was not working for you. Therefore, there is nothing that will happen that can make things better. The best way to recover from abuse is for you to block all forms of communication.

If you have joint custody of children, you may not be able to wipe this person entirely from your life. It is therefore advisable to create a strict custom contract, according to which you only communicate on matters regarding your children using third-party channels exclusively! Otherwise, ensure that you have set up court orders for all forms of agreements.

Think about the extreme trauma bonding, the gross abuse, and the addiction you had to the narcissist. Sometimes the best way is for you to accept that the only way you can recover from such damage is to pull away and cut your losses once and for all. Think of abstaining as a way of protecting yourself from hurt. In other words, each time you initiate contact with your abuser, you are handing them the ammunition to blow you off.

Remember that you lived with them, and so they know what your weak points are and how they can wound you even more profoundly. It is not until we heal that we will stop forcing ourselves on the narcissist for love or craving them or even justifying to ourselves giving them a second chance. When we completely stop contact, then we can begin to heal.

Step 2: Release That Trauma So That You Begin Functioning Again

If we are going to heal, we have to be willing to reclaim our power. We have to do the exact opposite of what we used to believe; 'I can fix him/her, I will feel better.' Your power belongs inside you. The moment you take your focus away from your abuser, you will be able to channel that power into rebuilding your self-love and paying closer attention to making yourself whole again.

At first, it might seem like understanding who a narcissist is and what they do is essential. But the real truth is that these things cannot heal your internal trauma. What you need to do is to decide to let go of that horrific experience so that you can be at peace. You will begin to rise, get relief, and feel balanced again once you have decided to take your power where it belongs—inside you.

Step 3: Forgive Yourself For What You Have Been Through

When the insecure and wounded parts of us are still in pain, we often are pushed into behaving like children who are damaged. We often look for people's approval, and especially from our abuser, we hand our abuser the power to treat us as they see fit. And that's the time you realize that you have given them all your resources: money, time, and health. The most unfortunate thing is that while doing that, you end up hurting the people that matter the most in your life... your children, siblings, parents, and friends.

Yes, it might be hard to forgive yourself for this, but you can do that if you want to rebuild your life and everything you lost to your abuser. By working through your healing process, you will soon find resolution and acceptance. You can move away from lacking self-love and respect to living a life full of truth and responsibility, and well-being.

You will realize that when you forgive yourself, you acknowledge that this was all a learning curve, and this is the experience you learned, and hence, you will use that to reclaim your life. It is when you release your regrets and self-judgments that you can start setting yourself free to realize greatness in your life irrespective of what stage you are at. This is the point when you will begin to feel hope again, hope that will steer you forward into fulfillment and a life full of purpose.

Step 4: Release Everything And Heal All Your Fears Of The Abuser And What They Might Do Next

Do you know what bait to a narcissist is? -Anxiety, pain, and distress. These are the things that can perpetuate another cycle of abuse no matter how we tell ourselves that we have separated from them. It is indeed true that abusers can be relentless. In most cases, they do not like being losers. But one thing that you have to understand is that they are not as powerful and impactful as you may have thought them to be.

They need you to fear and go through pain so that they can function. Once you have healed your emotional trauma, they fall apart. Therefore, it is crucial that you become grounded and stoic by not feeding into their drama; this way, they will soon wither away along with their power and credibility.

Step 5: Release The Connection To Your Abuser

So many people have likened their freedom from a narcissist to that of exorcism. When we liberate ourselves from the darkness that filled our beings, we allow ourselves to detox and let light and life come in. If that light has to take over the shade, the darkness has to leave so that there is space for something new to come in. In the same manner, it is essential that you release all the parts that were trapped by your abuser so that you can tap into a more supernatural power, the power of pure creativity.

When you disentangle yourself from the narcissist, it is not just about cutting the cord; it is also about releasing all the belief systems you might have associated yourself with subconsciously. It is only then that you can break free to be a new person and not a target of a narcissist.

Even though it might be tempting to seek revenge on your abuser, this is something that you have to try hard to avoid. Rage has the power of pulling you back into deeper darkness and a game that your abuser is an expert at in the first place. The best form of revenge is one in which you decide to take back your freedom and render your abuser irrelevant.

And it is likely going to crush their ego, and they will be powerless and at a loss that they cannot even affect you. Often they are in despair when it hits that you are a constant reminder of their extinction. It is at this point that the cycle ends, and your soul contracts to allow love and healing in so that you can be whole again.

Step 6: Realize Your Liberation, Truth, And Freedom

Traditionally, we learn that loving ourselves is a very selfish act. However, when it comes to finding liberation and freedom from the hands of our abusers, it is a very critical step that allows us to take in the truth and let it set us free from captivity. Yes, it is something incredibly difficult to do, but it is a necessary step toward achieving liberation.

Society has taught us that we are treated by others the same way we treat them. However, this is a false premise because we get treatment according to the way we treat ourselves. In other words, the measure of love that we get from others is equivalent to what we feel about ourselves.

Therefore, when we open up to healing and recovery, we open the doors for others to love us in reality and in more healthy ways than ever before. It is this act that serves as a template by which we teach our children so that they do not carry around subconscious patterns of abuse that were passed to us. This positive modeling only starts when we decide to take responsibility for our happiness and freedom. We slowly become the change that we would wish to see so that we can let go of being someone's victim and stop handing other people our power.

In other words, we take back our lives by doing everything necessary to aid our inner healing irrespective of what the narcissist does or does not do, something that's now irrelevant either way. It is at this point that we can thrive despite what we have been through and what has happened to us.

So, What Do You Need To Learn?

Refocus

One of the best things that you need to learn from the whole experience is the dangers that are associated with holding on to emotional attachments. It is when you let go that you will be able to experience the power that comes with healing. Take time to release the bonds to your abuser so that you can refocus all of your efforts on building yourself and a new life.

Self-confidence

If you are going to live a life of greatness after your abuse, you have to be willing to start putting back your life together. You have to come out with self-confidence so that you can reclaim your old self and find an even higher power to steer you forward towards success and victory. Once you start experiencing self-love, it is then that you will be able to turn a chaotic life into one that has calmness and joy.

Mindfulness

One of the things that you need to learn is to be fully present in the moment. This is where your mind is not anxious about anything. It's the moment when you are calm and have clarity of thought and thought process. It is only then that you can learn some of the powerful tools and tricks that can bring you instantly to the present so that you can live a life full of purpose and adventure.

Chapter 9:
What Happens After Leaving an Abusive Relationship

A lthough being with a narcissist is a truly horrific and often traumatic experience, breaking free can lead to initial loneliness. You are so used to being with that person, being involved in their stories, games, and sense of companionship, even if it is a twisted and mentally- emotionally abusive companionship; that finally leaving and being free can leave you feeling empty. This is natural- we are all chalices waiting to be filled. We need connections, stories, relationships, and various realities to keep us feeling alive and fulfilled. So when you break free from the narcissist, you are essentially an empty vessel. What new stories are you going to create?

This is, of course, in itself a beautiful process and fundamentally part of your journey. To be alone is to be all one, content, free, and soulfully happy in your own independence. Once we remove attachments and stories which are no longer good for us, we provide ourselves the space and time for new stories, new realities, and frequencies of being. I once heard the saying that life is like music. Life can be equated with music. We do live in a universe, after all! So, loneliness can be overcome by filling yourself with new stories- ones in harmony with your best interests and the best possible expression of you.

Connected to this are a self-recovery, healing, and boundary plan. Boundaries are very important, but so is your personal re-discovery of self and self-healing. Below are five key and highly effective ways to overcome loneliness.

Passion Projects

Immerse yourself in a passion project. New hobbies, favorite pastimes, or creating a vision board to align with your dreams and aspirations can all be marvelous gateways back to your true self. Following your greatest joy allows you to overcome loneliness and heal from the sufferings caused by your narcissistic partner. Passion and fire are the sparks of life; they re-energize and revitalize your inner core, further enabling you to stop feeling isolated or cut off from the world. This is an unfortunate consequence of being the victim of narcissistic abuse or mind manipulation—you may feel disconnected from others on a profound level. Refinding yourself through a passion project is essential for your well-being.

Re-Finding Yourself ("Know Thyself!")

Have you ever heard of the saying "know thyself"? This is knowing yourself on every level; your intentions, goals, dreams, hidden motivations, and your personality in its entirety. We usually become lost and allow in the illusions and judgments of others when we do not know ourselves. 'The self' is the holistic part of being, the persona, characteristics, and beliefs that make us unique. It is our thoughts, feelings, subtle impressions, emotions, past experience, and deeper inner workings, also having a soulful aspect or significance. Recovering from a narcissist and refinding yourself tie in closely to knowing yourself or knowing thyself. Not only can taking steps to rediscover and know thyself help you overcome loneliness, but it will also help increase your self-esteem, self-worth, and personal confidence.

Meditation

As briefly delved into earlier, meditation is one of the most profound ways to heal from a narcissist. Feeling lonely is due to feelings of separation or disconnectedness, and these all stem from your mind and emotions. Meditating reconnects you to your true self, inner harmony, and a sense of peace and well-being. It also expands your mind and allows you to be an observer of any chaotic, destructive, or afflictive thoughts, beliefs, or emotions. During the many months or years of narcissistic abuse, you will have been through some terrible, manipulative treatment. You may have been gaslighted, made to feel small, weak or inferior, or generally insulted on repeat. Your feelings, opinions, and perspectives may have been overlooked, and where your beautiful qualities and strengths should have been supported, encouraged, and cherished, you instead received neglect and abuse. All in all, your partner knocked your confidence and self-esteem in many unseen ways.

These all have profound negative effects on your inner belief systems, psyche, and unconscious workings. Thoughts and emotions, which shape and define you as a person, are strongly influenced by experience and memories; so any abuse you may have suffered can become deeply ingrained. Meditation fills you with a "conscious emptiness," an empty space for new levels of thought, feeling, and awareness. You may be able to access your higher self and higher mind, feel better and more positive about your life, and see all negative happenings as an opportunity for growth and new wisdom. In short, feeling lonely is replaced with feeling empowered.

Self-Therapy

The importance and power of self-therapy really cannot be undermined or overlooked. Self-therapy is any type of therapy that can be performed at home or in our own time. It is great for the mind, body, emotions, and spirit. It is not just your thoughts and emotions which suffer during narcissistic abuse but also your soul, the core and hidden part of yourself. This is the part that allows us to feel love, empathy, a deeper connection to others and life's beauty; connect with music and access transcendental states, and develop advanced cognitive, intuitive, and emotional frequency functioning.

Self-therapy incorporates a wide range of choices and channels, so, fortunately, there is bound to be at least one route that works for you. Meditation, sound therapy, nature therapy, music, art, creative expression, spiritual literature, yoga, tai chi, massage, energy work, and mindfulness are all forms of self-therapy. In fact, many people can change their whole mindset through the self-love and care which comes with engaging in therapy. Choosing to give yourself a healing massage, listening to soothing and peaceful music, and going for a mindful walk in nature, or reading some soulful poetry can all be effective self-therapies in their own rights.

New Social Groups and Organizations

Balanced with all the other key ways to overcome loneliness and heal for the long term is the engagement of new social groups and organizations. This can include peer support, groups for victims of narcissistic abuse, or simply any organization or venture which allows you to feel good. Being happy and connecting with others is the best way to let go and move forward with your life, despite the initial loneliness you may feel. You can feel lonely or isolated in a group too, because the truth is loneliness is just a mindset. Some people feel lonely even when surrounded by family and peers, just as many feel most at peace and blissful when alone. True happiness and contentment come from your ability to connect and feel at ease with the world. Taking the first steps by putting yourself out there will re-spark your passion for life and connection and your connection with yourself.

Boundaries: Your New Power Word

Boundaries are your new power word! Breaking free and liberating yourself cannot occur until you put healthy boundaries in place. Not only do they need to be healthy, but they need to be strong, so there is no chance of magnetizing or attracting another narcissistic relationship into your orbit.

Let's look at all the ways to create, develop and maintain a boundary plan.

1. Positive Self-Talk and Power Words

Positive self-talk may not initially appear as a form of boundary creation; however, it is. Self-talk is the conversations we have with ourselves. When we engage in positive self-talk, we open new neural pathways and actively influence the neurons in our brains. These neurons are responsible for how we think, feel, and respond to people, situations, and experiences. They are also responsible for our communication, both internal, with ourselves, and external, through our interactions with others. Just through positive and mindful self-talk, a natural boundary is created due to the ripple effect thoughts have on inner and external reality. In short, an invisible energy field is created through the power of the mind, thoughts, and subtle intentions exhibited. This invisible energy field is your boundaries.

Connected to this is the effect of power words, specific words used with self-talk to enhance and amplify the power of your boundaries. Words can, in fact, be used, spoken, or thought like a mantra or affirmation for optimum effect. Neuroscientists have discovered the incredible influence thoughts have on our physical being, emotions, and overall well-being or vibratory state (inner frequency), and this is backed up by a number of other schools of thought. Neuro-linguistic programming, cognitive behavioral therapy, and many alternative therapies and healing modalities all recognize and support the truth that our thoughts are powerful shapers and creators of our world. It is not only inner currents that are affected but worldly reality as we know it. So, harnessing the power of your mind in your boundary goals will allow your personal boundaries to expand and grow stronger, assisting you for the better.

2.   Self-Affirmations

Connected to this are self-affirmations or affirmations. Self-affirmations are essentially affirmations that can be spoken or thought during meditation or any contemplative activity for great effect. They are best performed as a sort of ritual or daily integrated habit. Taking time to dedicate some minutes to affirmations daily will enable your aura, your electromagnetic energy field to be strengthened and expanded, and your mind strengthened. As the body is a complex and interconnected system, this has a profound effect on your emotions and thus increases your sense of boundaries on many levels. Mental boundaries, emotional boundaries, physical boundaries, and spiritual boundaries are real, and once you begin to truly develop your own boundaries, you will realize how 'one and the same' these all are. Once you strengthen one of your boundaries, you can protect yourself from harmful or destructive energy. This includes the intentions and attempted projections of your narcissistic ex!

To engage in self-affirmations effectively, make time for a daily morning and/ or evening routine. This routine creates a structure in your life and an almost 'ceremonial' aspect. This is precisely what affirmations are, a sort of ceremony-like meditation. Setting your intentions and committing to self-affirmations as a daily routine inevitably sharpens and strengthens your mind, further opening you up to new ways of perceiving. Included in this is protecting yourself and the connection this morning or evening routine has to self-healing and strengthening your aura.

3. Self-Healing/ Aura Strengthening

Kirlian photography has shown how there is an electromagnetic energy field surrounding each one us known as an aura to some. Spiritual beings, healers, and energy workers have been aware of this energy field or aura for quite some time; however, it is only in recent years that the science to support it has made itself known. All living entities have an electromagnetic energy field, from plants to animals and homo sapiens. This energy field is responsible for all thoughts, feelings, subtle impressions, beliefs, interactions, emotions, past memories and experiences, and one's general energy and vibration. We give off vibrations in every moment, and this is where the modern age term "vibes" has originated from. In terms of Kirlian photography, one's aura can be seen to show just how real subtle energy and influences are.

Chapter 10:

How Can I Recover from the Emotional and Mental Wounds Left by the Abuser?

N arcissists are opportunistic hunters. They will target whoever is in reach, but they prefer to seek out a challenge. When the intended victim is someone who is more settled in their own sense of self and is confident, outgoing, and spontaneous, they will present an even more tempting target to the pathological narcissist. Dodgson (2018) indicates that narcissists enjoy the challenge of taking down someone who will provide them with some resistance. It doesn't really thrill them to take power from a weak person; instead, they enjoy the thrill of taking down someone who is also dominant and strong. So, if you are the target of a narcissist or you have become their victim, do not doubt yourself and say it is because you are/were weak. Instead, you should focus on the road to recovery once you have left the narcissist or have escaped from the abuse.

Even narcissists who only occasionally gaslight you or only abuse you to a lesser extent can inflict some pretty horrific and long-lasting damage. You can't simply go on with your life and hope to heal. Chances are that you are damaged in ways that you are not even aware of yet, or if you are aware of how much the abuse has affected you, you may be too lost to find the road forward. In both these cases, you need a strategy or "a street guide" to help you find your way.

In planning your road to recovery, you may need to formulate a strategy–just like in chess–to help you cope and help you back onto your feet. Otherwise, you will remain the gaslighter's pawn long after they have left your life.

Why We Fall Victim

According to Dodgson (2018), narcissists enjoy targeting people who match their own perfect ideal; hence, they will go for strong individuals, especially people who take care of themselves on an external level. They may be attracted to beautiful, well-groomed, physically fit individuals. At first, they may see these people as their perfect partner or friend. However, that sadly does not remain the case, and they will systematically drain you of your power and what had at first attracted them to you until you are so torn down that you no longer appeal to them and then get discarded.

Empathically strong people are also prime targets for narcissists since they make the narcissist feel good by sharing their understanding with them. Narcissists thrive on people who try to help them. Karen Arluck, a psychotherapist (Dodgson, 2018), believes that narcissists target:

- People who are in some way impressive or admired
- People who compliment them or try to help them
- People who fit their perfect ideal
- People who validate them, try to understand them, and will not be likely to leave or quit on them

Contrary to popular belief, narcissistic abusers tend to go for strong people, not emotionally frail people (Dodgson, 2019).

Future Strategies

Narcissists want to drive you crazy with doubt and fear. They gaslight you to make you doubt your own grasp on reality. By developing an action plan and sticking to it, you can be prepared for future assaults by your abuser. When drawing up your action plan, you may want to consider the following areas to plan for:

- Set boundaries

It is important to know what you will ignore, what you will accept, and what you need to avoid. A colleague, who is a little self-centered and makes the occasional jab at you to bolster their own self-esteem, may fall into the "ignore" category; however, a colleague who engages in sexual harassment and then makes you feel like you started it or that you liked it, would definitely fall in the "avoid" category. Do not accept this form of abuse. Once you have set your boundaries, stick to them.

- Know your rights

Whether the abuse happens at home, at work, or in a social setting, you have rights. Know them. In most democracies, the rights set out in the Universal Declaration of Human Rights of 1948 apply. Interestingly, these rights were drafted due to the merciless and inhuman acts perpetrated by Hitler (a historical narcissist) during World War II. The following are rights that may be infringed upon by a narcissistic abuser, and you can use the powers of the law against such abuse:

70

- The right to say no to sex

- The right to privacy

- The right to be respected (to not be shouted at, not humiliated, or victimized)

- The right to dignity

- The right to safety and peace of mind

If you are suffering a violation of your basic human rights, you can seek legal representation and should know that you are protected by the law.

- Create consequences

Lancer (2018) writes that we need to set consequences that match violations of our boundaries. This is crucial since it can give you an instant way to act, instead of overthinking and then becoming confused and then overreacting. Just like the prior, long-winded sentence, which sort of loses the plot, you need to avoid an emotional run-on and the jumbled reactions that this creates.

- Support

Develop the guts to ask a friend that you trust to be your soundboard. In using an objective person to talk to about the manipulative patterns that the abuser is creating in your life, you can develop the ability to see their schemes and manipulations. Beware the isolation habits that narcissists and other emotional abusers perpetuate. They want to keep their victim all to themselves. You need to find supportive friends who can help to keep your mind in order.

Staik (2019) writes that people who repel narcissists are individuals who are supremely confident in themselves, and they leave no gap where doubt may creep in that may be exploited by the narcissist. They can see that the gaslighting is really about the narcissist and not about them. This allows them to avoid getting emotionally hurt by investing their emotions in themselves and not in the narcissist. They quickly let the narcissist know that they know what the abuser is doing. Remember that narcissists work on the sly, and once they are told (in no uncertain terms) that you know what they are up to, they lose interest in you since they know they will not accomplish anything.

To work effectively on your own recovery, you need to go beyond simply looking at the future (though this is essential too), and you need to heal the hurts you already have. Here's how.

- Forgiveness and Letting Go

Many victims of narcissistic abuse struggle to get back on their feet. They blame themselves for not seeing the manipulations of their abuser for what it really was—abuse. Inner Integration (2018) writes that this may have a lot to do with you suffering the effects of Stockholm Syndrome, where you identify more with your abuser than with yourself. You end up making excuses for the abuser, who holds such a central role in your life, and as a result, you feel like you were responsible for the abuse. To move on after the abuse has ended, you may need to first forgive yourself for any perceived "flaws" on your part. Affirmations are a great way to do this. If you begin to listen to your own thoughts, you may begin to hear echoes of your abuser's voice, and it is up to you to counter their voice and reclaim your own identity.

Here are some affirmations that may prove beneficial:

- "I am strong enough to move forward."

- "I forgive myself for caring about someone who did not deserve it."

- "I can love people who treat me with love and respect."

- "It is okay to say "No" to someone who does not have my best interests at heart."

In extreme cases, your emotional damage may have manifested biologically, actually changing the make-up of your brain chemistry. Indeed, it is quite possible to exhaust your feel-good chemical neurotransmitters like serotonin and dopamine. In these cases, you may require medical intervention, and this is not something to be ashamed of. It is not another way that you fall short—it is you taking care of your body and mind and acting responsibly.

If you do not forgive yourself for your role in an abusive relationship, you will not be able to move forward or let go. You need to face the fact that you made mistakes and that it is okay.

Forgiving yourself is about you letting go of your flaws and embracing your own life. It is essential that you make peace with yourself following an abusive episode so that you can move forward and let go of the negative effects of the abuse.

Sometimes you will need to face the reality that you may need to forgive yourself and your abuser to move forward. Remember that forgiveness is not the same as saying that it is okay. By forgiving your abuser, you are not giving them permission to inflict more abuse. Rather, it is you saying that you are now letting them go so that you no longer suffer continued abuse at their hands and at the memories of their abuse. This is how you let go.

Inner Integration (2018) also writes that for victims who repeatedly fall into the abuse cycle, they may need to delve deeper into their lives and find the original abuse that they suffered. Most often, the patterns of abuse started in childhood, and if you do not take ownership of that abuse and heal that wound, you will repeatedly fall back under a narcissist's spell.

Chapter 11:

What Are Some Ways to Heal Yourself After Having Experienced Emotional Abuse?

When you have emotional trauma, it becomes difficult for you to control your emotions. When in this state, the trauma survivor is left vulnerable that the slightest physical, sensory, and emotional cues cause panic as it reminds them of the abuse and trauma.

During this time, the body and mind activate the same way as if exposed to an existing threat. It feels confusing and terrifying to the trauma survivors when they experience this. Learning some grounding and self-soothing techniques help to regulate the emotions when panic sets in.

When you try these techniques, you can feel safer now as it enhances your calm state.

Benefits of Grounding Techniques

When you feel intense anxiety or emotions threaten to overwhelm you, grounding techniques help you remain in the present moment. Doing this will allow you to feel in control and know that you are safe, not back to the abuse.

Staying in the moment means you must focus on the physical world and the sensations you feel right now. You can use these skills whenever your emotions are wild or distressed after your emotions were triggered. During this situation, you become stressed by being caught up with the problematic thoughts and memories of your past encounters with the narcissist.

Reliving bad experiences can make you feel afraid, leading to the development of negative habits. Some of those habits include drinking, binge eating, sleeping, and addictions. These are opposites of healing, which you can prevent from happening through grounding techniques.

How to Do a Grounding Technique

It is easy to perform a grounding technique. When you feel panic or overwhelming emotions, focus on an aspect or sensation of the physical world. For instance, touch the ground or hold the hands of your friend. The impressions you get from these will focus on the internal thoughts and feelings that plague your mind.

When it comes to grounding techniques, you must always practice. Doing this helps you calm down naturally after getting upset. When performing your grounding skills, you must focus on the external experience or the outward appearance to let your negative feelings go. Practice different techniques to find out which one works well with you.

Some of the grounding techniques you can try include:

Physical Techniques

- Put your hands in the water, feeling its temperature from your fingertips to the backs of your hands. Try using warm water first, then cold water next. The alternating temperature helps you stay grounded.

- Hold an ice cube in your hands and feel the sensation as it starts melting. An ice cube is an excellent tool to use for grounding techniques with its coldness. It is particularly helpful when dealing with intense feelings.

- Touch or pick up items near you whenever you feel distressed or disassociated. Concentrate on whether it is light or heavy, soft or hard, or warm or cool to the touch. Guessing their colors based on the texture is also an excellent exercise.

- Take a short walk, focusing on your steps. You can concentrate on the feeling as you walk on the ground or silently count your steps. You may also take notice of your footsteps' rhythm each time you put down and lift your foot again.

- Deep breathing is also a grounding technique that helps you keep calm. Take a deep breath, slowly inhaling and exhaling while simultaneously thinking 'in' and 'out.' Feel your lungs getting filled with breath and the air getting pushed back out.

- Perform some exercises or stretches such as jumping up and down, jogging, or other similar activities that move different muscle groups. Notice how each movement makes you feel, keeping your focus on it.

- Savoring each bite of food or drink with you enjoying how they taste and smell. Let the flavors linger on your tongue. Concentrate on them to keep your thoughts away from your intense emotions.

- Take a seat or keep standing. Either way, you can stay now whenever you experience traumatic episodes by focusing on the awareness your body feels. Notice each sensation from head to toe. From the coldness of the glass you hold in your hand to the straight posture you keep your back.

- Listen to your surroundings. The barking of the dogs, the chirping of the birds, each grunt of a machine working, or the gentle thud of footsteps around you. Focus on the conversations you hear, the sounds of the rain pit patting on the roof. All of these helps you stay in the moment and not get lost in your painful memories.

Mental Techniques

- Consider one or two categories, such as mammals, places, girl's names, etc., and mentally list them. List as many items, or things you can think about that belongs to every category you included in the mental exercise.

- Try playing a memory game by looking at a detailed picture such as a cityscape for a few seconds. Take in all details of the photo, then put it face down while you recreate it in your mind. Recreate it as much as possible, or you can list in your mind all the things you can remember.

- Recite a song, poem, quotes, book passages, or anecdotes, anything you can remember. Do this in your head while visualizing each word or silently mouthing it to yourself while shaping every word in your mouth?

- You can exercise mentally with numbers, such as by reciting the multiplication table. You can also count from 1 to 100 or backward. Simple addition or subtraction problems are great as well.

Self-Soothing Skills

Learning some self-soothing skills can also help you stay calm and relaxed when reeling from the memory of narcissistic abuse. By soothing, it means regulating your consuming feelings, so you are back to yourself again. The idea is the same when your parents pat your back while you cry.

Only this time, you do it to yourself. There is a bit of a disadvantage with self-soothing, as you might use addictive behavior as a quick fix. It makes it crucial that you choose healthy things to help you cope with your trauma as self-soothing skills.

Use Positive Associations

The use of positive associations created while performing said grounding exercises could also help you with traumatic episodes. Use cue objects, words, or scents that you have associated with good or safe memories. When you see them or hold them while having an attack, they will remind you that you're safe.

Opposite positive associations, you can use distancing techniques when the cues you made began to have negative associations. These techniques will guide your cues back to safe visualizations. Both techniques may be enhanced when performed with meditation.

Deep Breathing

Breathing exercises have been known to be helpful when you need to calm down. When your emotions are overwhelming, focus on your breath so you can induce relaxation and centering. When you take a deep breath and release it, think of your stressors getting released with every exhalation.

While doing breathing exercises, you may indulge in some meditation or listen to soothing music as a background—both help keep you calm. Thanks to the music, you can stop distracting thoughts from entering your mind.

Containment Exercises

Whenever you feel pain because of intense emotions, you can use containment exercises to separate yourself from these feelings until you are ready to deal with them. With these exercises, you can regain your emotions as they allow you to choose when and where to process them freely.

Containment exercises are a lot like mental exercises. Visualize in your mind an actual container—strong and large—enough to safely hold all your traumatic experiences and painful memories. The container is tightly sealed, which can only be opened when you think it is safe.

The container serves as your locker where you can keep negative emotions throughout the day. You put them inside the box and wait until you dare to examine and process your hidden emotions. With this exercise, you can avoid becoming overwhelmed by anxiety, fear, and dissociation.

Chapter 12:

Effects of Gaslighting

G aslighting is a crazy-making effect that can lead to exploitation, which is sometimes hard to see. The intention of the person using gaslighting is to, in a subtle and organized way, crumble the self-confidence of the victim so that they are not able to act independently. In the end, the victim becomes a robot who only obeys the order of the manipulator.

The emotional damage caused by gaslighting can be enormous on the victim. When a person is exposed to gaslighting for too long, they lose their sense of self-identity, and they start to distrust their judgment and second-guess themselves.

Gaslighting may lead a victim to develop emotional and mental concerns. Self-doubting and confusion can add to anxiety, and this anxiety can lead to depression, post-traumatic stress, and codependency.

The effects of gaslighting can be detrimental to the victim; these effects don't come all at once; they come in three stages: disbelief, defense, and depression. Before we go into these stages, let's take a look at the harmful effects gaslighting has on victims;

Confusion

Gaslighting works when the victim is unaware of it, and the constant use of gaslighting tactics by the narcissist makes the victim gradually bend to their will. Over time, doubts creep into the victims' minds, and with more gaslighting going on, the victim is confused. Though they know something is going wrong, they can't pinpoint exactly what it is.

It is a never-ending cycle for the victims as long as they are in close relation with the narcissist. Confusion results from the narcissist's exploitation of the victim's vulnerabilities. Narcissists keep their victims always second-guessing what they throw at them as they are always alternating between acts of cruelty and acts of kindness.

The narcissists break down victims piece by piece to become more and more unstable, and eventually, victims come to rely on them for comfort and guidance as confusion takes its toll on victims mentally and physically.

Confusion in the victims eventually leads to isolation, as the victims are too confused as to how the whole situation came to be in the first place.

Loss of Confidence

When a person falls victim to a gaslighting narcissist, their confidence starts to erode, and as they may find themselves second-guessing things, the victim develops a heightened sense of self-doubt. Every decision will now be backed with an internal question, "What if I...?"

The victims start to live in fear of doing the wrong things as they are now sensitive to the constant projection, blame, lies, and humiliation of the narcissist. As a result of looking up to the narcissist for approval before taking action, they ask themselves, "Am I too sensitive....?' And because they act with fear, they often end up making mistakes in their activities.

As time progresses, the victim will start showing signs of low confidence; they would find it hard to offer a simple thank you when they are complimented. This happens because of the unconscious emotional damage caused by gaslighting: a victim will reject a positive view of themselves because they have unconsciously accepted the fact that they are unworthy from the narcissist.

A victim will find it hard to hold eye contact with others because they are afraid others will see right through them and notice their flaws. The narcissists have successfully projected a part of themselves onto the victim.

Loss of confidence also makes victims always apologize as they are never doing anything right in the eyes of the narcissist, and to prevent further name-calling and humiliation, they apologize even for the words they say.

Indecision

A typical result of gaslighting is questioning everything, as the victim doesn't know what's real and imagined. This, in turn, means the victim finds it challenging to make the most straightforward choices because they now find it impossible to know what is "right" from what is "wrong."

Victims of gaslighting not only have trouble making big decisions, but simple choices such as brushing their teeth are now also hard to make, as they have been caught up in the narcissist's web of illusion, and they are bonded to the narcissist.

This kind of bond to the narcissist is formed out of the fear that the victim will lose their sense of self. One part of the victim will try to align itself to the needs and choices of the narcissist, while another will try to align itself with the victim's preferences.

Moreover, the narcissist projects their fear of taking responsibility and the need for perfection onto the victim, so the fear of taking responsibility makes it hard to make decisions.

Gradually, victims begin to lose their power to make decisions until they cannot decide anything for themselves. Now they have to rely on the narcissist for guidance and ask the narcissist for permission to do things.

Distrust

As a result of the same victims of gaslighting feel, they try to cover up the fact that mental manipulation is going on in their lives, and when their family and best friends start to notice the changes in them, they deny the subject and cover-up, or they may avoid the issue.

Gaslighting victims start to withhold information from people who mean well because they fear what will happen if they were ever found out by the narcissist. They begin to withdraw from society, and they start to distrust other people.

The victims of gaslighting not only have trouble trusting family and friends, but they also increasingly feel they can't trust themselves either.

Distrust causes victims not only an inability to form new friendships and relationships but also to withdraw themselves into isolation from friends and family.

This particular effect of gaslighting continues to occur even after the victim has successfully eliminated the narcissist from their lives, as when they make new friends, they find it difficult to trust and will always be hypervigilant about relationships.

Melancholy

Gaslighting practiced on the victim over time will take away the happiness and joy of the victims. Narcissists leave their victims afraid, confused, lonely, and unhappy through mental manipulation and emotional abuse.

The victims have the feeling that they used to be a different person, one who was confident and carefree. What the victims don't realize is that anyone who lives under the constant oppression of the gaslighting narcissist can have character change.

This vile act compounds over time to cause a significant personality change in the victims: victims who used to be calm, fun-loving, and the best of themselves are now depressed due to the mental abuse.

Gaslighting causes depression in victims after a while, as the constant letting down, blame-shifting, dissonance, and mental manipulation take their toll on them.

The effects of gaslighting don't come all at once in victims; these effects occur in stages, and victims will go through three steps when they suffer in the hands of a gaslighting narcissist: disbelief, defense, and depression. When depression sets it, the victim discards their own reality, and the narcissist wins.

Stage One: Disbelief

Disbelief is the first reaction of the victim towards gaslighting behavior. They can't figure out what is happening and why the narcissist suddenly changes their attitude towards them. Of course, the narcissists want this because, along the way, they know the victim will submit to their wishes, and they will control the victim's reality.

At first, the narcissist presents a different version of themselves to the victim. In the eyes of the victim, a narcissist is a person full of love, and they will find it hard to believe that a person that has once shown love to them is now something else.

This first stage is a state of total unawareness on the part of the victim. The victim is not aware of the gaslighting that is employed by the narcissist. All that they see is that the narcissist who once supported them and shown love to them is now very critical of them, and any attempt to talk about the reason for the change of attitude is blocked or diverted into something not relevant to the reason why their attitude changed or in worse cases the attempt to talk is met with silence.

At this stage, love-bombing stops, and nitpicking starts: the victims are shocked about the narcissist's radical change of behavior. One minute, the narcissist was the perfect person, and now the narcissist is a shadow of their former selves.

The victim will still try to make sense of everything at this stage and might attribute the sudden change of behavior to another event in the life of the narcissist.

Stage Two: Defense

At this stage, the victim still has a grip on the part of themselves to fight and defend themselves against the gaslighting manipulation.

The narcissist at this point is gaslighting with covert threats, triangulation, and name-calling.

The narcissist is trying hard to make the victim think they are insane at this point, but a part of the victim is working hard to believe this while another part has accepted the fact that the victim is crazy.

This is the stage where gaslighting tactics begin to work, but the victim still has control over a little part of their mind. At this stage, gaslighting has worn out a part of the victim's mind; the victim begins to mentally weaken and starts to give in.

In any case, the narcissist's gaslighting starts to do what it is expected to do, that is, to startle the victim by creating self-doubt and guilt in them. This emotional harm causes the victim, after some time, to lose their sense of the real world and their sense of self. They become lost and incapable of trusting in their own memory. The victim may start to feel shame, and after a while, the victim will feel they are in great danger.

Psychologists believe that nature has built-in coping mechanisms from birth for when we feel we are about to be destroyed.

One of these coping mechanisms is explained as "Stockholm Syndrome," where the victim adapts to the traumatic situation by unconsciously reverting to childhood patterns of behavior and bonds with their abuser as they did with their mother in their childhood when they feel threatened.

Another coping mechanism is "Cognitive Dissonance," where the victim seeks to rationalize the narcissist's behavior.

To defend themselves, victims do two things to cope with the gaslighting:

They rationalize the behavior of the abusive narcissist, and as such, they fall into a state of cognitive dissonance. This is a state of discomfort that occurs when a person holds contradictory ideas or beliefs in their minds at the same time.

Stage Three: Depression

At this stage, gaslighting has taken its full effect, and the victim has now become a shadow of their former selves. They begin to think they can't make decisions anymore; they can't deal with reality any longer, and they withdraw into depression.

By this stage, the victim can barely recognize themselves, and they are rapidly turning into a shadow of their former selves, living inside a war region where they are controlled physically and battered emotionally. The victim starts to avoid people, places, or thoughts and develops a lack of interest in activities that give them happiness and joy. They also begin to relive past experiences.

Chapter 13:

Narcissist Abuse

We are going to explain how narcissistic personality disorder comes to be. This will give you some insight as to how your abuser may have gotten to where they are today. That being said, it is important to understand that most people with a narcissistic personality disorder do not believe they have anything wrong with them. Therefore they very seldom seek treatment. If they do, it will likely not be because you pressured them into it. It is suggested that you use this as an opportunity to understand, rather than as a tool to attempt to show your abuser that they are abusive and to pressure them into seeking treatment.

Causes of Narcissism

Typically, personality disorders are caused by a complex series of issues that lead to the disorder developing. It is hard to predict or determine whether a child will become a narcissist, though there are some things that are believed to contribute to the development of the disorder. Here are the three theories of what goes into the creation of a narcissist.

Theory One: Environment

The first theory involved is their environment. Psychologists and psychotherapists believe that a child's environment can contribute to the potential development of personality disorders, including narcissistic personality disorder. The primary area in the child's environment where these disorders tend to develop is directly in the parent-child relationship. Typically, excessive admiration or excessive criticism toward the child can promote the development of narcissism. If a child is raised by a parent who is a narcissist, they may also learn the behavior and begin to express themselves with narcissistic behavioral patterns. In this case, the person may be on the narcissist spectrum but may not have a full-blown narcissistic personality disorder.

Theory Two: Genetics

As with the majority of illnesses, personality disorders can be inherited by family members. If an individual has one or more people with narcissistic personality disorder in their family, they may be at a higher risk of becoming a narcissist later in their own life. Although this may be an inherited characteristic, there is no way of testing genetics to determine whether or not a person will become or is at risk of becoming a narcissist in their lifetime.

Theory Three: Neurobiology

Neurobiology refers to the connection between the brain, behavior, and thinking. Psychologists, neurologists, and other researchers believe that an individual's neurobiology may encourage them to develop narcissistic personality disorder at some point in their life. Again, there is no way to test a child's brain to determine whether or not they are at risk of developing narcissistic personality disorder in their lifetime. Some theories believe that traumatic life events early in life can change the individuals' neurobiology, thus making them more likely to become a narcissist later in life. This can happen as a result of the trauma itself or because of the way their parents may change their behavior toward the child. For example, if the parents' divorce is traumatic to the child and the child becomes neglected by one or both parents, this can contribute to narcissism. Alternatively, if the child experienced a loss or a personal trauma, such as a serious illness or injury, and one or both parents coddled the child long after the injury attempting to protect them from further dangers, this could also contribute to the potential onset of narcissism later in life.

Risk Factors

Many will not receive a diagnosis because they genuinely believe that there is nothing wrong with them and it is everyone else who has a problem. Despite this being the prime age for diagnosis, some children may begin to show narcissistic traits as they are growing up. Some of these may be typical to their age and will never go on to develop narcissistic personality disorder, whereas other children will.

Anyone can be a narcissist, no matter what their age, gender, religion, or ethnic background may be. The disorder is not related to the demographics of the individual so much as one or a combination of the causes listed above.

The general consensus agreed upon by doctors and psychologists is that the biggest risk factor leading to the potential development of narcissism later in life is parenting. Parents who are neglectful, overindulgent, abusive, or pathological have a tendency to treat their children in a way that results in the child never actually overcoming the grand sense of self that all children have. In general, children are expected to be more self-indulgent because this is how they learn about their own identity and how they fit into the world. As they grow older, this sense of self-indulgence should fade away over time as they find their answers and begin fitting in. For those who have not been raised in a household where they had access to healthy parenting, either as a result of excessive or neglectful parenting or as a result of constant traumatic abuse, are at risk of not growing past this self-indulgent behavior. Instead, they use it as a way to feel good in spite of their parents' leading them to believe that they are unworthy of love, or as a way to continue feeling good as a result of their parents leading them to believe that they are special over everyone else and deserve to be treated as such.

Complications

There are many complications that an individual will face if they are diagnosed with narcissistic personality disorder. Of these complications, the majority of them are rooted in social behavior. Individuals with narcissistic personality disorder struggle to maintain relationships, have difficulty at work or school, and may resort to drug or alcohol misuse. The narcissistic personality goes untreated, and in many cases, even when it is addressed. This is because, in most cases, narcissists are incapable of admitting and accepting that they are narcissistic. Doing so would result in their entire reality crashing in around them. Furthermore, transitioning from a self-serving lifestyle that others feed into as a result of their abuse and into one that requires them to think of anyone other than themselves is virtually impossible. The amount of pain and loss they would feel from this transition would be more than they are willing to endure. The only time a narcissist may actually seek support is if they have literally lost everyone in their life and are no longer able to reel people into their abuse cycle. In this case, they may be willing to consider therapy. At that rate, therapy is not guaranteed to be effective as they may just use this as a bargaining chip to confirm that they are "doing better" when, in fact, they are not.

Another major complication that narcissists face lies in shame. As a result of their upbringing and how they were taught, every single narcissist faces shame in their childhood. Where this shame comes from depends on what caused their narcissism in the first place, but it virtually always results in them feeling the need to "delete" their true self in favor of a false persona. This behavior essentially supports the narcissist in splitting away from the aspects of themselves that they are ashamed of and supports them in creating a mask that they feel should fix what has caused the shame in the first place.

If the narcissist was raised in a neglectful household, the shame would lie within virtually every aspect of the narcissist. As a result, the repeating feeling of shame and neglect would create a sense of trauma in the child that would cause them to want to discard any aspect of themselves that brought them shame or, in their opinion, resulted in them being neglected. Their true self: the parts that they were ashamed of and that they feel lead to the neglect, would then be denied in favor of a false self or mask that would ultimately redesign their profile and make them seem likable to everyone.

If the narcissist was raised in an overly coddled household, the shame would lie within any aspect of the child that was not coddled by the parents. So, if they were deemed an academic genius, anything they struggled with that made them feel as though they were incompetent or uneducated would cause shame. They would become addicted to the praise and the attention they received when they were behaving according to their parents' standards and would feel ashamed about any aspect of themselves that did not live up to what their parents felt was acceptable. This would either be aspects of themselves that contradicted what the parents were proud of, or any aspect of themselves that were ignored or even punished out of them by the parents. The true self, then, would include all of those aspects, whereas the false self would seek to discard them in favor of being entirely likable and admirable to their parents.

If the child was abused growing up, any number of aspects of themselves could bring them shame. This can be even further amplified and reinforced if the abuse experienced by the child was also narcissistic abuse. In general, these aspects will directly relate to what they felt caused the abuse. This could lead to a wide range of aspects of themselves that they would then want to discard or decimate in favor of becoming a different variation of themselves that would be void of all of the aspects that they felt lead to their abuse in the first place.

Many complications can arise in the face of the shame that narcissists feel. Because they blame this part of themselves for the pain and trauma they experienced at various points in their childhood, they feel strongly about the need to hide the true self in favor of the false self, which they feel will earn them greater respect and better treatment from everyone else. Because they embody this false self entirely, this leads to their sense of believing that they are special: because in their eyes, unlike everyone else, they have worked so hard to discard the "bad" parts of who they were.

Prevention and Treatment

Preventing and treating narcissistic personality disorder is challenging since the majority of these individuals will never become properly diagnosed. If the disorder is related to parenting styles, the parent may be unwilling to admit to there being a problem as well, creating further difficulties for the child to get the required care. Still, some preventative measures and treatments are available for narcissistic personality disorder.

Chapter 14:

Coping with Narcissist Abuse

I f you have ever been in a relationship with, or are experiencing narcissistic abuse, then you probably know how hard it is to leave. You know what you need to do, you think about how you can escape, and you gain the courage to do it, but then, you don't. You don't because something holds you back in. You sit there and think of all the good memories, then think about what would happen after you actually left, then you think about all the things that haven't happened yet, and wonder if things will change if you stayed due to whatever excuse you come up with. This is another form of fear. Your mind has you trapped as a result of the abuse to the point where, when you do decide to or try to leave, you feel a flood of panic. The fear is something many of us can't seem to overcome, so we stay in the relationship hoping that things will get better or that things will be okay. But it never does, so you start from the beginning, getting ready to leave again. It's a vicious cycle that no one should have to go through. If you find yourself sitting there most of the time asking yourself, "should I stay, should I go," then you most likely already know the answer to this and should go. Things don't get better; they only repeat themselves. The narcissist you are involved with will always make promises they can't keep, and they will always build you up for the main purpose of thrashing you down.

Devastation is difficult to manage, but with the right support, you will get through all the stages and reach a point where you view your ex as a person you knew but has no hold over you. I promise you that if you reclaim your power after getting through the dark side of your breakup, you will come to a realization that without sacrifices, you will stay stuck. No one likes to be stuck, and no one needs to feel the way you do right now. So, get up, release yourself, and become one with who you are by starting the first stage of the breakup.

Devastation

So, we have already talked about devastation, but did we talk about ways to get through it the easiest way possible? No. When we are devastated, we don't want to do anything, eat anything, speak to anyone, and we would rather drown our sorrows under cozy blankets and cry into our pillows. Devastation comes in a few different stages and can come all at once or one by one. First (or last) comes the shock that you are actually done, that your relationship is actually over. Memories will pool inside your mind and flush you back to what was. Next, you may feel numb or cry (a lot), with the feeling of not caring about anything. Your eyes may hurt, you may not be able to sleep, which makes you unable to concentrate on anything, and you could withdraw from the rest of the world because you would rather do this alone than have anyone see you as pathetic as you feel. Next, anger sets in. You may become bitter to people around you and forget to take care of your needs, like clean the house or get dressed. Anger will consume you if you let it, but this is part of the process of healing. To get past this feeling, you feel like a "rebound" will help you get out of this slump. So, you put on a fake smile, get dressed up, and go out on the town to get under someone else, so that you feel the affection you crave so much. This is called denial. You are in denial about your feelings. You think you are ready, but you are not. If you do this, you will most likely end up with the same type of person you were just with, thus resulting in more damage to yourself later down the road.

As much as devastation hurts, and you may want to do everything to stop feeling that aching pain in your chest. The best way to get through this stage is to learn techniques that will help you deal with these overwhelming emotions. It is important to remember that although this stage is needed for a successful final stage if you let yourself feel this way for too long, you will never recover. So, instead of remembering your lowest point, reminiscing about the good and bad memories, remembering all your fights and all your efforts, or trying to come with answers to why you were so badly treated, stop. If you continue to do this, the pain only escalates and keeps you in the devastation stage longer than you need to be there.

Instead, try these tactics to help you speed up the process of devastation:

1. Closure

This stage of devastation may be so hard for some people that they often go back to their spouse during this stage. After all the crying and the anger, maybe a couple of rebounds, they decide to go back. This is not healthy because the next time you leave, you will have to start this process all over again, and I don't need to remind you what happens to our brains when we are under this type of stress. So, just end it. If you have made the decision to leave, then do that. Get your closure, write letters (send them or don't), say your goodbyes (physically or to yourself), and do whatever you need to gain some sort of closure. But don't go back.

2. Externalize

It revolves around knowing and understanding how you feel and being patient with these feelings. It's about accepting the hurt that you feel but not clinging to it. Knowing that there will be better days, and right now, it is okay to let it all out.

3. Appropriate process

This is a necessary process to help you cope with the devastation because it allows you to make sure you are not obsessing over the breakup and your feelings. It comes in five steps:

> Admit the pain or anger
> Vent, and let it out to the people who are most supportive - or write about it.
> Determine your response to your emotions (are you going to sit here and feel sorry for yourself, or are you going to try to get up and take care of yourself today?)
> Stick to your goals, and your plan to recovering and making it through this first stage of devastation
> Forget it. Shift your thoughts to something else, something more positive. You can only learn to forget once the other steps are taken care of.

4. Distraction

Devastation will destroy your sense of accomplishment and hold you from doing things you used to enjoy. This stage in the process is to fight back - do the opposite of what you feel. So, if you feel like sitting in bed all day, get up and sit on the couch or go outside for the day. Distract your mind with telephone calls to loved ones, play crosswords, exercise, write, draw, etc. Do something creative, and don't allow yourself to sit with this pain.

5. Maintain your schedule

Whatever your routine was before, continue with it. If it is hard to fully maintain a routine right now, just do a couple a day, then gradually increase your strength to move on to the next thing you used to do. For example, if you used to wake up and go for a run, come home, shower, get ready for work, go to work, come home and make dinner, then read a book. Start by just getting up and going for a light walk and having a brisk shower. Day by day, increase your routine to one more thing on that list.

6. Find a place that doesn't trigger you.

If your breakup consisted of them moving, and you are stuck with all the memories no matter where you look, consider moving or staying with a friend for a while. If you had to move, and it hurts to go out and see the places you guys walked or went on dates, avoid these places and find somewhere new to go. Just don't avoid it forever.

7. Give in to the need for closeness without sexual contact.

The fastest way to get through this stage is physical closeness. So, if you have a child, cuddle them; if you have a best friend, ask for lots of hugs. When you need a shoulder to cry on, reach out to someone you trust. Along with this physical closeness, bonding with people you trust is a bonus in this recovery.

8. Avoid all things sexual

Although physical closeness is essential for recovering from a narcissist breakup, sexual entanglement with someone can make things worse. If you haven't completely moved on, you may feel shame, guilt, and even more anger. We want to avoid this as much as possible.

Devastation is the first stage of recovery, and it may also be the hardest. However, when you make it through this stage, you can move on to start taking better care of yourself, which will make you feel good. In short, you must let your feelings sink in, don't fight them, take care of your well-being, and stay off the internet or forums (at least for now). The last thing you want to do is overwhelm yourself with research that reminds you of your narcissistic relationship.

Allow Yourself to Grieve

Believe it or not, crying and tears are beneficial to your recovery. Crying is scientifically proven to rid your body of stress. When you let your other emotions in, this also helps with the grieving process. However, if you hold your emotions in, you are making connections in your brain that suggest holding it in is a better solution and will actually cause more problems for you later. When people hold their tears and anger in, they never learn to release or let go. Instead, they teach themselves that it is okay to hold it in, which can result in an outburst later. Have you ever cried so hard, then after you get this foggy feeling, but it feels as though a weight has almost lifted? This is because you have relieved yourself of the tension or stress that you feel.

Chapter 15:

Complex Post-Trauma Stress Symptoms

P ost-traumatic stress disorder is a result of some type of traumatic event. You've probably heard about it associated with war veterans, but it can also be caused by physical assaults, rape, car accidents, or emotional abuse. Really, any kind of disturbing or upsetting event that occurs can result in PTSD, particularly if it overwhelms your ability to cope with what happened. What's more, women are twice as likely to suffer from PTSD, and they also experience a longer duration of symptoms and more sensitivity to any triggers that remind them of the event. PTSD, as you've probably commonly heard of it, happens after a single traumatic incident, but there is another form, called Complex PTSD or C-PTSD, that results from repeated trauma over months or years. This is the type of PTSD we'll be talking about, though both types of PTSD share similar symptoms and treatments.

The effects of C-PTSD can be drastic if left untreated, and aside from the mental health implications of the condition, it can also lead to physical health problems. You might suffer from headaches, stomach problems, and sexual dysfunction, among other things. What happens with C-PTSD is that you do not only remember what happened; it's as if you're back in the incident you endured. It's like you went back in time and are living through that moment again. Your body responds as if you are too, and in response to it, the body produces the stress hormones that result in a whole range of physical, mental, and emotional symptoms.

C-PTSD in Women

Women who are suffering from the effects of C-PTSD often don't seek help, sometimes for years, and then, when they do, the condition is frequently misdiagnosed or missed altogether by the health professional. It is also not uncommon that the woman herself may not be aware of the problem.

Women tend to internalize their problems, and rather than look outward to their situation, they might just decide that what they're suffering from is just a product of their own personality, thoughts, and emotions. They don't realize that there is a concrete problem from which they're suffering. For that reason, it's important to understand the causes, symptoms, and treatments for this condition. It's hard, though, because there is still a stigma against most mental health disorders, and that's particularly true for women who suffer from PTSD following an assault or C-PTSD following years of emotional abuse. Moreover, women are frequently traumatized further by the professionals in whom they confide. They might be questioned about the veracity of what they're saying and their reaction to the situation.

Differences in PTSD and C-PTSD Between Men and Women

As with many diseases and conditions, there is a difference in how women experience C-PTSD compared to men. Women, for example, are more likely to experience depression and anxiety while also having more difficulty feeling and dealing with their emotions.

Additionally, they often avoid activities and things that remind them of what happened to them. Alternatively, men are more likely to turn to alcohol or drugs to mask their emotional response to trauma.

The key to treating C-PTSD is to be educated about how it can affect you. It is a treatable condition, but you first have to recognize that you have a problem. This can be difficult for women since they frequently feel a need to be perfect and are often reluctant to admit they have something that they perceive as a weakness. It's not just their perception either; women are constantly told they need to do it all and must do it well. That's an unrealistic expectation and can create rather intense pressure. Before we talk about some of the treatment options for C-PTSD, let's look at some of the more common symptoms for women and men.

C-PTSD Symptoms

For C-PTSD to be diagnosed, a patient must experience symptoms for at least a month, though they could be suffering for months or years before going for a diagnosis. Symptoms might not appear immediately, either. When they do, they can typically be categorized into three types:

1. Re-experiencing the trauma, which typically occurs in the form of intrusive and distressing recollections of a single event or multiple events. These recollections could come in nightmares or through flashbacks.

2. Emotional numbness and avoidance of places, people, or activities that remind the individual of what happened to them.

3. Increased arousal, which can result in difficulty concentrating or sleeping, as well as feeling jumpy and being easily irritated and angered.

Typically, the traumatic events that cause PTSD, in general, include exposure to actual or threatened death, serious injury, or sexual violation, but trauma also occurs with long-term emotional abuse, where the individual's fight or flight response was repeatedly stimulated, eventually resulting in complex-PTSD. In this situation, the brain doesn't distinguish between physical trauma and emotional trauma; it only reads your fear and responds accordingly. It also tends to read anxiety as fear and responds with a cascade of physiological responses, including the production of stress hormones. The chronic production of stress hormones has dramatic physical and emotional effects. It's also important to note that the threat or abuse doesn't have to be directed at the individual involved, and both kinds of PTSD can also result when someone witnesses a traumatic event or emotional abuse. The specific symptoms for a diagnosis in each of these general categories include the following:

Re-Experiencing the Trauma

Re-experiencing trauma can take the following forms:

- Spontaneous, recurrent, and involuntary memories of the traumatic event that intrude into an individual's consciousness. For example, experiencing a memory can happen when a trigger is perceived. In children, this might be seen in how they play. Their play may take the form of themes or aspects of the trauma they suffered.

- Recurrent and distressing dreams related to the traumatic event- This might mean dreaming specifically about the event, but it can also just be dreams that have a feeling similar to it. In children, this may take the form of dreams that don't have any recognizable content.

- Dissociative reactions—such as flashbacks—where the individual experiences the memory as if it were actually happening again- This typically causes the individual to become fully immersed in the flashback.

- Intense, prolonged psychological distress from being exposed to either internal or external triggers that symbolize the traumatic events.

- Specific physiological reactions to reminders of the trauma they suffered. For example, some individuals might become nauseated when stimulated by a reminder of what they suffered.

Avoidance of Distressing Memories

This is a more typical response for women and can be diagnosed based on the presence of two or more of the following symptoms:

- An incapability to recall certain significant aspects of the traumatic event that cannot be accounted for by a head injury, alcohol, or drugs.

- Persistent and often exaggerated negative beliefs or expectations about oneself, other people, or the world in general. For example, the person might say, "I am bad," "No one can be trusted," or "The world is a dangerous place."

- Persistent feelings of self-blame or blaming others regarding what caused the consequences of the traumatic events

- Persistent feelings of fear, horror, anger, shame, or guilt

- Diminished interest in participating in significant activities

- Feeling detached or estranged from other people.

- A persistent inability to experience positive emotions

Changes in Arousal and Reactivity

This can occur in both men and women and can be diagnosed based on two or more of the following changes:

- Irritability and a marked increase in aggression

- Reckless or self-destructive behavior.

- Hypervigilance.

- An exaggerated startle response.

- Problems concentrating.

- Significant distress or impairment in social or occupational areas of functioning that cannot be attributed to the effects of medication, drugs, alcohol, or some kind of medical condition like a traumatic brain injury

Treatment Options for PTSD and C-PTSD

There are several treatment options available for both kinds of PTSD that have been shown to be effective for helping women cope with their symptoms. These include both psychological and medication-based treatments. The first step in treating PTSD (either kind), however, is to diagnose the condition. To diagnose PTSD, your doctor will begin with a physical examination to check for any medical problems that might be related to your symptoms; this is to rule out the possibility that your symptoms are caused by other conditions and not PTSD. Once those physical ailments are ruled out, the doctor may refer you to a psychologist for an evaluation. That will involve talking about your symptoms and the events that likely produced them. Finally, the psychologist will make use of the diagnostic criteria listed in the Diagnostic and Statistical Manual of Mental Disorders (DSM-5).

A diagnosis requires that you were exposed to trauma either directly, as a witness, or through learning someone close to you was traumatized. Additionally, you might have been repeatedly exposed to graphic details of a traumatic event, as might be the case with first responders. Along with exposure to the trauma of some kind, your symptoms must have been persistent for more than one month, and they must create significant problems in your ability to function in the different areas of your life.

Normalizing involves the following:

- Recognizing and accepting that physical pain may be a symptom. People with either kind of PTSD can struggle with migraines, back pain, or stomach and digestive issues.

- Recognizing and accepting that flashbacks or nightmares might occur and that they can be triggered by sounds, smells, or even a phrase that someone else says.

- By normalizing the symptoms, it can help alleviate the patient's sense of guilt. The treatment is still a long process, but it begins with hope. The goals of the treatment program include helping you regain a sense of control over your life by utilizing the following strategies:

- Teaching skills to address the symptoms as they occur.

- Helping you think more positively about yourself, other people, and the world in general.

- Learning better coping strategies for symptoms.

- Treating other symptoms related to the traumatic experience, like depression, anxiety, or substance abuse.

Chapter 16:
Letting Go and Moving On

Whether or not you feel like you have been the victim of narcissistic abuse, being in a relationship with a narcissist is not without its challenges and may lead to an unhappy end, or rather, it could lead to you staying in it, even when it contradicts who you are as a person and your dreams and goals of successful relationships and a happy life. Whatever you are feeling at this moment as you read this book, letting go of your relationship may not feel like your first choice, and that's okay.

For some readers, there is no question that it is time to pack up and go. It all depends on a person's wants and needs and their ability to be honest with the truth of what is really going on in their marriage or partnership. It can take some time to understand the dynamics of your narcissistic partnership after you have identified that you are in one.

Moving forward can be a challenge, and many people will struggle with putting an end to this type of relationship, mainly due to the reality of narcissistic abuse and emotional manipulation. It really is about who you are, what your experience is, and what is going on right now to help you understand the best choice forward for you.

The following will help you identify when it might be good to leave a narcissistic relationship and how to put an end to it so that you don't keep coming back to it and repeating the same patterns repeatedly. A lot of that experience requires getting help and support and eventually a period of recovery from the narcissistic relationship so that you don't end up with the same type of person again, repeating the patterns in an entirely new relationship.

When and How to End the Relationship

The time is right for you to leave if you have undergone any emotional, mental or physical abuse, if you have identified serious cycles of manipulation or narcissistic issues that never change, if you are sacrificing your own personal power, integrity, success, and desires, or if you feel like you are being taken advantage of on a regular basis to support someone else's fantasies of who they are. There are a lot of ways that narcissism from within your relationship can affect your quality of life, your personal views, your self-worth, and more, and it is not worth it to stick around hoping that your partner will change and be more what you need. They don't care about what you need. They will only ever care about what they need.

If you have tried for a long time to help your partner identify their issue and help them "heal" their problem to no avail, then it is time to let go and move on. It is important to recognize that you can never heal someone for them; they have to do the work to heal themselves. Being a supportive partner is always a good thing, but if you are familiar with how your patterns of support have enabled your narcissistic partner to stay in their preferred role and behavior patterns, then you need to admit that you are at the end of the rope so that you can heal on your own terms and find a happier lifestyle.

The stages of detaching from your partner can go on for a while as you begin to identify the issues and start to pull away, changing your role in the situation and recognizing your readiness to end things. It can be uncomfortable for your partner, who will make it uncomfortable for you as a result, and so understanding some of the stages that you will likely go through will help you prepare for moving on.

Detachment from a Narcissist: Stages

First Stage:

When the rose-colored glasses come off, and you stop accepting blame, guilt, or shame in your relationship, you begin to resurface and "wake up" to what has really been going on. In the first stage, you are "seeing" more clearly all of the patterns, the covert and subversive ridicule, and all of the tools of manipulation to push you away and punish you, and then pull you back in and adore you. This is the stage of awareness of the problem and the first shift and change in the situation.

Second Stage:

You may still have feelings for your partner at this point, even a seriously deep love bond; however, your usual desire to please them no matter what will begin to be replaced with the feeling of anger and even resentment that they are so consistently and continuously demanding of your admiration, adoration and pleasing them. The love may still be there, but you are not so "naïve" anymore.

Signals of the Second Stage:

- Your partner's lies no longer have an effect on you and feel obvious and pathetic.

- You are no longer succumbing to the manipulation tools.

- You regain a sense of self-worth and feel you deserve to be treated better.

- You begin to fight for yourself more and create more conflict with your partner.

- You begin to regain and rebuild your self-confidence and self-esteem.

Third Stage:

Your confidence is being reborn, and you feel better about yourself and your choices. You may have already joined a support group at this time or started to see a counselor to help with your growth and are feeling more empowered emotionally and mentally. You can better focus on your own wants and needs and start seeing how life would be if you are not involved with your narcissistic partner.

Signals of the third stage:

- You cannot stand to be around your partner.

- You no longer feel an obsessive love or strong love bond.

- If they begin to push your buttons or act inappropriately, you will either have no reaction and not care or retaliate and lash out against them.

- Enjoy more time with friends, in support groups, engage in classes or group meet-ups that support your interests

- You will start to make decisions to support yourself without concerning yourself with your partner's preferences or interests.

- You will begin to make your move to let go and move on by planning your out and getting your ducks in a row.

Fourth Stage:

This is the end of the relationship when your focus becomes facing your future without your partner. At this point, you may have cut the cords, moved out, separated, begun the divorce proceedings, etc. This is the stage when you will have cut them off and out of your life and when you can begin to feel new and like yourself again. You will not want anything to do with your partner, and in some cases, you may have to maintain some kind of contact (if you have children together).

The Overall Process of Letting Go and Moving On:

This process won't occur for anyone overnight. You can end up living in the cycle of one stage for a long time until you are resolved to move forward into the next stage. Being stuck in these processes is highly common, and there is a way to help you ease through a little bit better so that you don't stay stuck for longer than you need to be.

As you begin to consider letting go and moving on, hang onto those thoughts and let yourself feed into them. You are allowed to imagine your life differently, apart from your partner, and it can help you to build steam and momentum if you continually consider the process of cutting cords and stepping forward. It helps to keep fueling your self-esteem and doing things that will help you support yourself in the process. Follow these steps to help:

1. Think about it. Let yourself fuel your exit with self-esteem building and thoughts about moving on. Build momentum so

that you can keep revisiting why you are having these thoughts to begin with.

2. Use a journal or a notebook to write out all of the experiences you want to have, the life you want to live, the places you want to go, and where you want to be successful in your life. Start to write down and consider the kind of partnership and partner you would like to experience. You can even jot down all of the aspects of your current relationship and then make a comparison between what you have and what you really want. Getting into the habit of journaling about you and what you want can help you refocus your life goals and ambitions and further motivate you to let go of the relationship that is hurting your choices and chances for a healthy and successful life.

3. Reflect. Explore your relationship and ask yourself what part, or role, you have played in the experience. The narcissist may be manipulative, toxic, and cunning, but it certainly always takes two to tango, and so it might help you to be honest and identify what ways you have supported the toxicity of your relationship. How have you not lived up to your own standards of love and life? How have you enabled this behavior? What can you do to shift these patterns? Spend time with these thoughts and truly reflect on your own energy in the relationship. Write it down in your journal and begin to create awareness about your role in the partnership. You don't want to fall for the narcissist again, and knowing where you fall for the traps can help you resist them in the future.

4. Find supportive literature. There are countless books out there that aren't just about overcoming a narcissistic relationship, but that are also about empowering yourself, finding the career of your dreams, learning new skills and hobbies, and so on. You can begin to reclaim your identity and your sense of pride and joy in your life by seeking out self-improvement books and literature that will empower you and give you strength.

5. Spend time with others. Connect with your family, friends, co-workers, support groups, etc., and talk about it. Feel free to be yourself around your network of loving and supportive people to help you feel that you are not going to be alone when you walk away and move forward.

Chapter 17:

Maintaining a Healthy Relationship

I f you are already in an unbalanced relationship and want it to change, check out some of these tips.

Take A Good Look At The Relationship

Is it worth pursuing? Is it unbalanced because you no longer love and respect each other? Is it because you've grown apart?

In addition to answering those questions, you have to recognize that certain behaviors like:

- Swearing or yelling at you

- Harassing statements that are directed toward you

- Interrogating or degrading you in any way

- Attacking your self-esteem and that of your loved ones

- Blaming you for the things that go wrong in his or her life (or in general)

- Extreme jealousy

- Gaslighting

- Threatening you in any way (specifically physical or sexual abuse)

- Threats to your family members or friends

- Threats to your kids or pets

- Controlling behavior

- Isolating you from your loved ones

- Controlling you with money or any other means

are not healthy.

Be Clear & Honest With One Another

If you want something to change, you can't lie to the other person or hold in your feelings. You have to offer up your feelings and allow your partner the same respect. Use "I statements": "I feel that..." "This behavior makes me feel that I..."

Not only that, offer up examples of why you feel this way. Don't just give him or her general statements. The more specific, the more of a chance that you'll get a positive change

Consider The Option of "Miscommunication"

Sometimes, things are not how we perceive them to be. If you think that your partner isn't being considerate because he isn't texting you back when you ask questions or because you always have to come up with the plan of action, consider this:

He might just be clueless. I'm not making excuses for your partner. I'm just urging you to be communicative and open-minded. It could just be a horrible, horrible case of miscommunication.

Keep In Mind That We Shouldn't "Change" People

We can't change anyone. They have to be willing to change themselves. You can't force someone to act the way that you want – especially adults. We can change the way we do things, and we can express how we feel and what we need. However, it is up to your partner what he or she wants to do with that information.

Try To Restore Balance To Yourself First

We have to treat ourselves with respect before we expect others to respect us. This is a statement that we often take for granted. We expect others to immediately be respectful toward us, but we don't take care of ourselves.

Reflection is an important step in fixing any relationship. Look within yourself to find what you can do to be happy. Listen to your instincts and trust them. Be open to what your reflection reveals about you and what you need. Find healthy stress relief techniques and treat your body right. These things will lead to a happier life and will lead you to a happy relationship.

Insecurity and Jealousy

Some people may say that the reason for their behavior is insecurity and jealousy. This is not an excuse for treating anyone in a cruel or abusive manner. However, if you deal with insecurity and jealousy at their roots, you can control those behaviors. Counseling will help with these, but there are some things that you can do at home. The first step is to recognize insecurity and jealousy.

Insecurity is a lack of confidence or assurance. You can also call it self-doubt, anxiety, or a lack of confidence. If you are feeling insecure, there is more of a chance that you will develop unhealthy levels of jealousy while you are in a relationship.

There are many different types of people, and we all handle our insecurities in different ways. We can categorize most people into six different categories based on how they handle what they view as their shortcomings:

- People who take those insecurities as a challenge (to better themselves so that they can overcome them),

- People that use humor as a defense mechanism,

- People who just surround themselves with positivity and pretend that they don't have any insecurities at all,

- People who lie about themselves in order to cover up any insecurities (I mean, outlandish wild tales!),

- People who verbally doubt themselves and put themselves down, and

- People who act out because of their insecurities in order to cover them up.

Most of us strive for the first category but end up falling into one of the latter ones. That doesn't mean that we can't change, though.

The Most Important Relationship That You Should Rescue

The most important relationship that should be mended after you leave an abusive relationship is your own relationship with yourself. You need to be able to fix the damage done to your self-esteem because of all of that emotional and mental abuse. Because of that, I want to talk about what you can do to build your confidence:

Self-confidence is a trait that we all take for granted. We rarely think about the ways that self-confidence helps us in our daily lives. One of the most important ways that it helps us is by helping us overcome our fears.

When we improve and build up our self-esteem and confidence level, it can really help us pursue our dreams. We will all fear certain things in our lives. Sometimes it is a phobia buried deep in our subconscious (fear of the unknown, the dark, clowns, being alone, etc.). Other times, we can easily overcome some of our fears by building up our strengths and by being confident in ourselves.

Let's talk about how we can do that. How we can build up that self-assurance so that we can be happy with ourselves is the first step to being happy with your life. Here are some simple steps that you can take to start that process. Mind you, you don't have to do these in any order.

Choose a couple off of the list to try first. If it doesn't work immediately, give them about a week to really have an effect. Keep up with the ones you feel most comfortable with, and drop the ones that aren't working for you. This is your life and your happiness. Do what feels good (and healthy) for you.

1.   Become a master at something.

Learning, practicing, and pursuing things that you feel passionate about helps to liberate your mind while focusing it on something specific. This practice will help you focus on other things as well. Practice makes perfect, right?

Studies have shown that it takes approximately 10,000 hours before we can master a specific skill. That is a lot of practicing and a lot of time to focus your mind on a specific task.

If you use this practice time with a task that inspires you, it is time well spent, and you will find it easier to focus. Don't know what activity or skill to choose? Answer some of the questions below to help you zone in on what you feel passionate about:

- Are you a creative person? Do you like to create things with your hands?

- Have you always wanted to try a particular sport or physical activity?

- What hobbies do you enjoy doing when you are by yourself?

- Which of your skills are friends and family members always commenting on?

- Is there something that you enjoy doing, which you would also be inclined to create? For example, are you an avid reader? Would you like to try your hand at writing a book?

2. Play dress-up.

When you feel presentable, and when you dress nicely, you can feel like you're ready to take on the rest of the world. You don't have to go out and buy something expensive or fancy. Casual clothes can be presentable too. You have to find the balance between comfortable and well-dressed.

Creating your own sense of style can help increase your confidence level too. Bring out your personality in your clothes. Don't be afraid to think outside of the box – as long as it goes with the dress code at work. If you're not interested in being fashionable or focusing on your appearance at all, just keep in mind that it's not bad to be known for having a clean and professional appearance.

3. Create an image of how you picture yourself.

When people say that you should "dress for the job that you want, not the job that you have," what they mean is that you should create a self-image of success.

If you can and if you have the software, create an image on your computer. Place yourself in the position that you want to be in five years from now or fifteen years from now. These mental images that we have for success are great ways to motivate ourselves to work harder and work better. Making these mental images into visual and tangible images that you can reference every day will make you feel great.

4. Squash those negative thoughts.

Negativity is your worst enemy. Be aware of how you talk about yourself and how you think of yourself. Negative thoughts can be anything from "I want to quit this" to "I look and feel gross today." The first step to stopping negative thoughts is to recognize this type of self-talk.

The second step is to visualize yourself actively stopping these types of thoughts from entering your mind. You can picture anything that works for you, including (but not limited to):

- Picturing these thoughts as water and stopping them with a dam inside your head,

- Imagining these thoughts as bugs and squashing them with a big boot or a stiletto heel, and

- Visualizing these thoughts as cannonballs and shooting them far away.

Conclusion:

Emotional abuse can be every bit as damaging as physical abuse. In fact, the scars can last longer, and it can take longer to identify since there are many ways for a partner to be emotionally abusive. Often they will dress it up as care and concern, but, in fact, it's all about control. For whatever reason, they feel the need to control your life and destroy your self-esteem and question your own emotional health.

Many emotional abusers have suffered similar treatment at the hands of parents, friends, family, or colleagues, although not all abusers were themselves victims of emotional abuse. Whatever the reason for this behavior, it is not acceptable, and you do not have to tolerate it, although it can be very difficult to escape from, since the abuser may not even realize they have a problem, or if they do, they may be unwilling to change.

It is possible to recover from emotional abuse and be happy again, as long as you can let go of the past and decide on new boundaries and expectations for future relationships. You can be happy again – and indeed, you deserve to be!

As we end this book, I would like to reiterate some points in recovering from Emotional Abuse:

1. The first step is to recognize the problem and then find out as much information about emotional abuse as you can from books and the Internet.

2. Do not hesitate to seek help from a qualified counselor, therapist, or support group, and be prepared to ask a lot of questions.

3. It is imperative that you always tell your friends and family what is going on, even if they are not very sympathetic or understanding. If they do not know, others may expect them to know or be afraid they will become a victim of Emotional Abuse – especially children! The more evidence of the problem there is, the more likely it will be that someone else will take action on your behalf if you are still experiencing it by yourself.

4. Seek professional help if things do not improve, or your abuser becomes more aggressive as time goes on – which is often the case. Most abusive people are totally unaware of the damage they cause. If you tell them you want to make a change, it's not always easy for them (even if they are willing) to change their ways, especially without professional intervention and close supervision.

5. The same applies if you are still experiencing other forms of abuse at the same time as Emotional Abuse – it is not uncommon for perpetrators of all types of abuse to engage in more than one form at once, although there may be some differences in intensity and severity between the different types.

6. If you are still experiencing Emotional Abuse, there is no need to let it continue. Never be afraid to speak the truth about what is happening in your life, and never do anything that you

feel uncomfortable about or make you want to undo an action later on.

7. Do not give up: there's always hope.

Well, you have reached the end of our journey through this book – a journey that has helped hundreds of thousands of people recover from Emotional Abuse and get their lives back on track! I hope it has been helpful, and I wish you the very best in your recovery and future relationships.

CPSIA information can be obtained
at www.ICGtesting.com
Printed in the USA
BVHW091932270521
608295BV00001B/186

9 781914 527593